CONTENTS

continued on the next page

GRADES 3–6

SPACE

HANDS-ON ACTIVITIES, THE LATEST INFORMATION, AND A COLORFUL LEARNING POSTER

by Mary Kay Carson

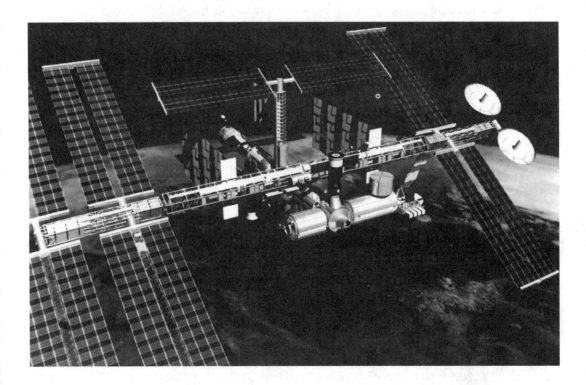

SCHOLASTIC
PROFESSIONAL **B**OOKS

New York ◆ Toronto ◆ London ◆ Auckland ◆ Sydney

**Consultant: Gregory L. Vogt, Ed.D.
Crew Educational Affairs Liason, NASA
NASA Johnson Space Program
Houston, TX**

Cover design by Vincent Ceci and Jaime Lucero

Text and interior design by Ellen Matlach Hassell
for Boultinghouse & Boultinghouse, Inc.

Interior illustration by Rosiland Solomon and Manuel Rivera.

Photo research by Joan Beard

PHOTO CREDITS Cover: Sun: NOAO; Astronaut: NASA; Shuttle: NASA; Neptune: JPL; Saturn Rings: JPL **Interior:** p. 1: NASA; p. 7: NASA; p. 9: NASA; p. 10: NOAO; p. 20: NOAO; p. 21: NASA; p. 22: JPL; p. 23: JPL; p. 24: JPL; p. 30: NASA; p. 31: AP/Wide World Photos; p. 32: NASA; p. 33: NASA; p. 34: JPL; p. 35: NASA; p. 39: NASA; p. 44: NASA; p. 45: NASA; p. 46: NASA; p. 47: NASA; p. 54: NASA; p. 55: NASA; p. 56: top—Lockheed Missiles and Space Co., bottom—NASA; p. 60: top—AP/Wide World, bottom—AP/Wide World; p. 61: top—NASA, bottom—AP/Wide World; p. 62: top—AP/Wide World, bottom—UPI/Bettman; p. 63: top—NASA, bottom—AP/Wide World; p. 64: top—NASA, bottom—NASA; p. 66: NASA; p. 70: NASA; p. 72 NASA; p. 73: NASA.

ISBN 0-590-60344-2

A NOTE FROM THE AUTHOR

Dear Teacher,

I can think of no other subject with more fuel to fire your students' imaginations than space. Why? Because in space, extraordinary things are possible: Yellow clouds made of poison float around Venus, astronauts push a 1,000-pound satellite out of the shuttle bay with one finger, and serious scientists write messages to aliens.

Space exploration is a new field with lots of as-yet-unanswered questions. Your students' guess about what's inside a black hole would be about as good as that of scientists at the National Aeronautics and Space Administration (NASA). It's your students' generation that will crack many of the mysteries of space. Astronauts and space scientists are the great explorers of our time. They lead lives just as remarkable, controversial, and tragic as those of Captain Cook, Columbus, and Magellan. What they discover changes the way we see ourselves and our small blue planet.

This book is organized into five main sections. Each section begins with general information about a space topic and is followed by a variety of student activities and reproducible pages related to that topic. Each section also has a take-home activity labeled SCIENCE TO GO. These activity pages allow your students to explore space topics further on their own or with their families. You'll find a color poster, accompanied by activities in the book's center. I hope you and your students enjoy these space explorations.

Sincerely,

Mary Kay Carson

Mary Kay Carson

Earthrise over the Moon

CHAPTER 1

WHAT'S OUT IN SPACE?

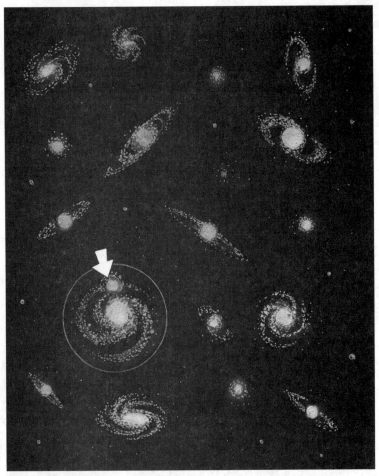

The Milky Way in our Supercluster

Our Place in Space

The universe is big. There are more galaxies in the universe than people on Earth. And each galaxy shines with the light of billions of stars. Between those stars are planets, comets, asteroids, and black holes—not to mention a whole lot of empty space. Just where do we fit into all this vastness? Our small, blue planet Earth is the third planet from the Sun. The Sun and its nine planets make up the solar system. Our Sun is a star, just like any other. Our Sun along with other stars belong to what's called our local star group. It includes our closest star neighbors like Alpha Centauri and Sirius. Our local star group—of which Earth is a part because we circle one of its stars, the Sun—is in the Milky Way galaxy. The Milky Way is a spiral-shaped galaxy with wispy arms that spin out from its center. (Other galaxies are shaped quite differently.) Our local star group lies in one of these arms called Orion. The Orion arm is toward the edge of the Milky Way galaxy, about two-thirds of the way from the spiral's center. The Milky Way itself is only a tiny part of a grouping of galaxies called a supercluster. These superclusters form chains and ribbons of worlds within worlds across our corner of the universe.

The Moon

Not everything in space is as mind-boggling as a supercluster of galaxies. What's the biggest and brightest thing in the night sky? The Moon. At about a quarter of the size of Earth and a mere quarter of a million miles away, the Moon is big and near. In fact, it's so close to us in size and distance that strangers to this solar system might at first think that Earth and its moon were double planets. After getting a closer look, they'd see how different they are. The Moon has no atmosphere, no water, and no life. For the most part, it's a still, dead world that doesn't change.

No atmosphere means there's a permanent, black, nightlike sky on the Moon—as well as no air to hold in heat or filter out solar radiation. So it's either very cold or very hot on the Moon. Daytime temperatures climb into the 250°F range and plummet to 290°F below zero at night. By the way, "daytime" lasts about two weeks on the Moon and is followed by two weeks of dark "night." The surface is a fine powdery gray-brown dust lying still in this silent, windless, and waterless world. The lunar landscape is peppered with countless craters that are up to 100 miles across. There are ancient seas of hardened lava and huge rocks the size of houses.

There is no life on the Moon, and except for infrequent impacts of high-speed rocks and dust, it is geologically dead as well. There aren't any active volcanoes, "earthquakes," or crustal plates floating on a molten core, as on Earth. There was never life on the Moon, but the young Moon was active geologically. Lava flowed from volcanoes and left the sealike depressions called *maria.* These "seas" of hardened lava remain after millions or even billions of years. The Moon's craters were caused by meteoroids and asteroids crashing into the surface. Many craters are still intact after millions of years. Some rocks brought back from the Moon's surface by the astronauts were found to be more than 4 billion years old! Most Earth rocks that old are buried far beneath the surface, covered by weathered rocks, changing seas, and a mobile crust. But there are no such forces on the Moon, so its surface remains unchanged. Today those 25-year-old astronaut footprints in the moon dust look as if they were made yesterday.

The Moon from Apollo 11

The Moon, our only natural satellite, completes a revolution, or orbit, around Earth about every 28 days. The Moon orbiting around us as Earth itself revolves around the Sun means that different amounts of shadow and reflected sunlight are cast toward Earth. The result is an ancient way of marking the passage of time—the phases of the Moon. Earth's stronger gravity has locked the Moon into a pattern of both spinning on its axis and completing an orbit in about 28 days. So as

MOON FACTS

From Earth:	238,000 miles
Day (one spin):	About 28 Earth days
Year (a trip around Earth):	28 Earth days
Orbiting Speed:	35 miles per minute
Gravity:	85-lb. kid weighs 14 lb.
Size:	2,170 miles in diameter

the Moon orbits the Earth, it spins just enough to keep the same side facing us. The result is that we always see the same side of Moon. No one knew what the Moon's "other" side looked like until a spacecraft flew around it and radioed back pictures in 1959. It turns out it's quite different from "our" side. There are many more craters but few dark *maria*.

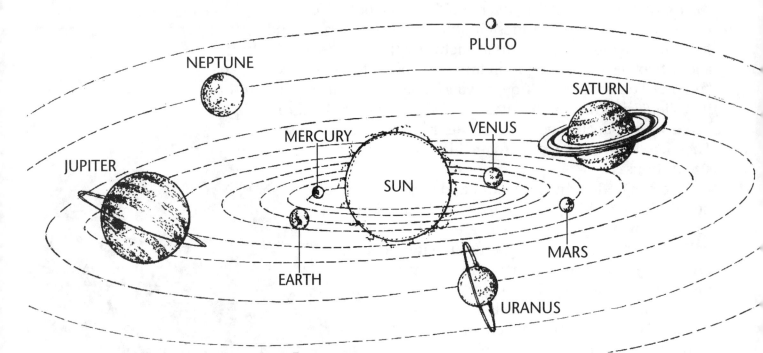

The Planets

When you look up at the night sky, some of the the brightest "stars" are actually planets. The planets may look similar as they reflect sunlight toward Earth, but the nine worlds that inhabit the Solar System are really very different. Jupiter, Saturn, Uranus, and Neptune are huge balls of mostly gas and liquid that have up to 17 moons each. The other smaller solid planets can be frozen, like Pluto, or baking-hot, like Mercury and Venus. But all the planets are ruled by the Sun's gravity. The Sun's gravitational pull keeps the planets in a path around itself, just like Earth's gravitational pull keeps our feet on the ground, as well as the Moon in our orbit. All the planets spin as they go around the Sun.

The Earth completes a spin *(rotation)* on its axis approximately every 24 hours. A complete spin is one day, by definition the time from sunrise to the next sunrise. Earth completes an orbit *(revolution)* around the Sun in about 365 days, or one year. The farther a planet is from the Sun, the longer it takes to complete the orbital path around it and the longer is its year. For instance, Mercury's year lasts 88 Earth days, and a year on Pluto is equivalent to 248 Earth years.

FAST FACT

Spinning is one way that space objects remain in stable orbit. Telecommunication satellites that orbit Earth also spin.

The Sun

Our Sun is a middle-aged star, average in size and brightness. But it's by far the main attraction in our solar system. This glowing ball of mostly hydrogen gas makes up 99 percent of the solar system's matter. A million Earths could fit inside the Sun. Scientists think that when the Sun was forming 4.5 billion years ago, leftover bits were thrown off as the Sun spun. Those bits remained in the grasp of the Sun's gravity as they later cooled and melded into the planets.

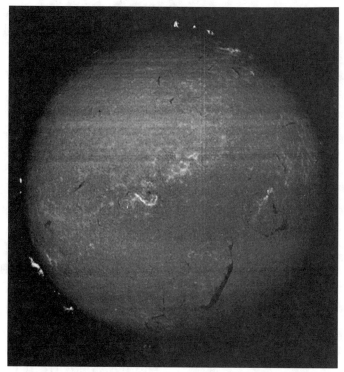

The sun displaying its solar flares and sunspots

The Sun's hydrogen and helium gases are the fuel for a furnace that burns at 29,000,000°F in the Sun's core! The furnace's energy is released when hydrogen is fused into helium by the high temperature and pressure inside the Sun. (This is nuclear fusion.) The released energy moves outward toward the Sun's surface where the temperature cools to 11,000°F. Heat, light, and other kinds of radiation continue to move outward from the Sun and into the solar system. The Sun's light and heat make life possible on Earth. Plants make their food with Sun-dependent photosynthesis. And all other life is dependent on plants or plant eaters. The Sun's hydrogen fuel is only half used up, so it will be a while before it burns out. Some scientists think Earth will be uninhabitable because of a dying Sun in about 5 billion years.

Sunspots are dark, "cool" patches on the Sun's surface. Some are as big as Earth. Solar flares are streams of electrically charged hot-gas particles escaping the Sun's surface during giant storms around sunspots. When these particles reach Earth and hit the outer atmosphere, the gas glows—just like the gas in a fluorescent light tube glows from electricity. Solar flares and storms can interfere with radio, TV, and even power transmission because they affect Earth's magnetic field. Most equipment is now built to prevent this. Sunspots, and the flares and solar windstorms that go along with them, come and go in an 11-year sunspot cycle.

FAST FACT

Scientists predict that as the Sun uses up the last of its energy, it will actually burn hotter until the last of the fuel is gone.

Starry Starry Nights

Stars are faraway suns, hot balls of gas and dust that give off, or radiate, their own light. (Planets and moons only reflect light.) Our galaxy is made up of about 100 billion stars. Stars come in different colors and sizes. Cooler stars are red; hotter stars bluish-white; and in-between stars yellow, like the Sun. Stars live and die. Every 18 days or so a new star is born in our galaxy. When a star dies, its material becomes very tightly packed, or dense. Sometimes when a giant star dies, its own gravity is so strong because of its density that it drags everything in toward itself—including light. What's left is called a black hole.

Star distances are measured in light-years. Light travels at about 186,000 miles a second, so the distance light would travel in a year is about 6 trillion miles, or one light-year. Our nearest star neighbor, Proxima Centauri, is about 4.24 light-years away, that's more than 25,440,000,000,000 miles! The Sun, by comparison, is only about 8 light-*seconds* from Earth. So whereas it takes 8 seconds for the Sun's light to reach Earth, it takes more than four years for us to see Proxima Centauri's light.

OUR STAR NEIGHBORS

Star	Distance from Sun (in light years)
Proxima Centauri*	4.24
Alpha Centauri A and B*	4.34
Barnard's Star	5.97
Wolf 395	7.7
Lalande 21185 A and B†	8.2
Sirius A and B†	8.6

*Proxima Centauri, Alpha Centauri A, and Alpha Centauri B make up the Alpha Centauri star system.

†Two stars close together, called a binary star system.

From Earth, stars appear to twinkle because of pockets of warm and cold air in the atmosphere that distort their light. Stars don't twinkle out in space. Falling or shooting stars aren't stars at all, they're traveling space rocks—meteors—burning up as they enter our atmosphere. Stars rise and set in the sky like the Sun and the Moon, because Earth is spinning. Their positions change with the seasons because of Earth's tilt.

FAST FACT

The North Star is used as a year-round guiding light because it hardly moves. That's because it's directly over the North Pole as Earth spins on its axis.

Constellations are names used originally for groupings of stars that seemed to form patterns in the sky. The stars aren't necessarily close to one another out in space. And the brightest stars aren't necessarily the closest. Other than our Sun, the brightest star in our sky is Sirius, which is actually twice as far away as Proxima Centauri. Sirius is just much larger.

Milky Way with meteor

ACTIVITIES

Fun With Phases (Science)

Model how light, movement, and shadow result in the phases of the Moon with your students. Divide students into pairs.

MATERIALS for each student pair

orange (or another sphere, such as a soft rubber or Styrofoam ball)
◆ sharpened pencil ◆ flashlight

DIRECTIONS

1 Stick the pencil into the orange so it becomes a giant lollipop.

2 Draw a big X on one side of the orange. This marks "our" side of the Moon, the side we always see.

3 Explain that the orange is the Moon, the flashlight the Sun, and the student holding the Moon will be Earth.

4 Darken the room as much as possible. Ask student Earth to stand in one spot, holding the Moon by the pencil high above the head. Student Sun then shines the flashlight on the Moon from a few feet away, as in the illustration.

5 Have student Earth pivot, holding out the Moon, until the Moon is directly between Earth and Sun. Ask: What phase is the Moon in now? (*New moon. The side of the orange that faces Earth is dark.*)

6 Earth now pivots around 180 degrees until the student's back is toward the Sun. (Make sure Earth is holding the Moon above the head!) Ask: What phase is the Moon in now? (*Full moon. The side of the orange that faces Earth is now completely lit.*)

7 Now have Earth pivot very slowly counterclockwise until the student sees a third quarter phase, then a crescent, and back to a new moon. Have Earth continue turning counterclockwise until it is clear that an entire lunar cycle has been completed.

8 Students Earth and Sun switch roles.

SCIENCE TO GO ▶ Challenge students to keep a Moon Diary for a month, sketching the Moon's shape every other night and observing its changes.

New

Crescent

First Quarter

Full

Third Quarter

Crescent

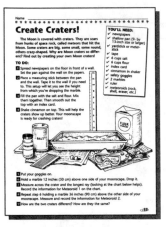

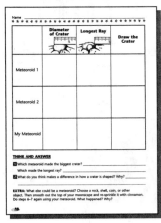

Create Craters (Science, Math)

The Moon is a pockmarked place. There are countless craters that range from the microscopic to the size of a city. Show students photos of the lunar surface and ask how they think the Moon got that way. Moon craters are the result of meteoroids and asteroids that hit the Moon millions of years ago. Discuss meteoroids and asteroids with students. Where did these hunks of space rock come from? Remember that the Moon is moving fast, and meteoroids and asteroids just get in the way sometimes, like bugs hitting a windshield. Do they ever hit Earth? *(Sometimes.)* Explain that craters have a raised edge, or *rim*, and spokelike *rays*. Ask the students why they think the Moon's craters come in so many different shapes and sizes. The Create Craters reproducible on pages 17–18 shows students how to make their own Moon craters under controlled conditions and helps answer this question. (The reproducible lists materials and detailed directions.) Distribute a copy to each student. Have students record their data on the reproducible.

Extension Activity Invite the entire class to pool their data on the board to see how much variation there was (useful if students are studying averages or division). Redo the experiment but change the variables; for example, use sand instead of flour or superballs instead of marbles, or toss marbles from an angle. Ask students to predict what will happen before they test their ideas.

The Scale of the Solar System
(Science, Math)

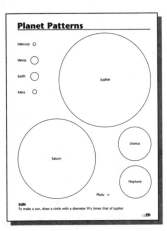

Help students comprehend the scale of sizes and distances in the Solar System. The Planet Patterns on page 19 provide the scale of the planets. You can photocopy and paste them onto cardboard for a mobile. (The sizes can be doubled or tripled.) Or use the sizes as a guide for choosing appropriate spheres as models. Ask students to bring in balls, marbles, round dried seeds, etc. Then challenge groups to match the approximate sizes of the Planet Patterns to what they have to make and label a model of the planets. Models can be displayed in class.

The planets' relative distances from the Sun can also be modeled. Find a fairly clear wall that's at least 13 feet long. Mark the distances shown on the From the Sun chart on page 13 with a pencil or tacks. (If there is no such wall available, you could use the ceiling or the hallway, or divide the distances in half.) Tape the planet names near their marks, or hang name tags from the ceiling. The Planet Patterns on page 19 could be used with the distance chart, but note that those planet sizes are NOT to scale with the distances on the chart. A model of the solar system with distances and planets on the same scale wouldn't fit into a classroom—that's because if the Sun were the size of a baseball on home plate, Pluto would be a grain of sand just outside the ballpark! Reducing the Planet Patterns by half would be less inaccurate.

EXTENSION ACTIVITY Students can research what the planets look like and then appropriately color the Planet Patterns. As a math tie-in, challenge students to model the distances on a different scale. For example, if the Sun were positioned at one end of the gym, where would the other planets lie? Students can double and halve the numbers until they get to the scale they want, or older students can set up ratios.

FROM THE SUN

Planet	From Model Sun*	Actual Miles from the Sun**
Mercury	1.5 in.	35,898,000
Venus	3 in.	67,084,000
Earth	4 in.	92,752,000
Mars	6 in.	141,575,000
Jupiter	21 in.	482,546,000
Saturn	3 ft. 2.5 in.	884,763,000
Uranus	6 ft. 5.5 in.	1,785,000,000
Neptune	10 ft. 1 in.	2,797,892,000
Pluto	13 ft. 3 in.	3,663,700,000

*Numbers have been rounded to the nearest half inch.
**Average distances. Most orbits aren't perfectly circular.

Tour the Solar System Fact Cards
(Science, Math, Language Arts)

Pages 20–24 are double-sided fact cards of the Sun and planets. Photocopy and distribute the pages to each student. Have them assemble the cards by cutting them out and folding on the dashed line. The cards can be pasted to cardboard or heavy paper to make them more durable.

The planets were named after ancient Roman and Greek gods, which is also where the symbols came from. The planet's size is its diameter, or distance across. (For example, the diameter of an orange can be determined by cutting it in half and measuring the distance from one edge to another.) Make sure that students understand day and year as explained in the information section. The orbiting speed is how fast the planet travels on its path around the Sun. The color is what it looks like from space, usually due to the light-scattering effects of its atmosphere. Gravity is the pull of that planet, explained here in terms of how much an 85-pound person would weigh (weight = mass × gravity). Life, or evidence of life, has never been found on any other planet or moon.

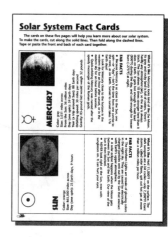

Play Planet Trivia!
(Science, Math, Language Arts)

There are lots of numbers, facts, and figures in the fact cards. Help your class process all the information with a mock quiz show. Divide the class into teams of 4 or 5 students. Give students some time to come up with 10 questions (with answers) from information on the fact cards. Examples might include: Which planets don't have moons? How many planets have days longer than ours? Which planet is about the size of the Moon? Encourage them to think of tough questions—it's their classmates who will have to answer them! The groups then take turns in round-robin fashion asking one another the questions, gaining a point for each correct answer. Keep score on the board. If a group can't answer a question after one minute, give the next group in the circle the chance for the point.

Students can also play Concentration with the cards. Have them cut their cards apart and lay out all the halves facedown. Then they take turns with a partne, turning a card over and finding its match. War can be played with the picture side of the halved cards also. Two students combine their decks and set the criteria for winning each round: size, speed, distance from the Sun, etc.

EXTENSION ACTIVITY The class can make a wall chart of the planet information, complete with color drawings of the planets. It will complement any model they've made.

Invent an Alien (Science, Critical Thinking)

No signs of life have been found on any other planets—yet. But what if extraterrestrial life were found someday? What would it be like? Would creatures on a low-gravity world need less bone and muscle to hold themselves up? Would a thicker atmosphere mean no lungs? Challenge students to choose a non-Earth planet from their fact cards and design an alien creature that lives there. Ask: How would it be adapted to its home world? Encourage them to learn about the planet's conditions from their mini-books. Have them label their paper with the creature's name and its home planet, as well as explanations of the form and function of its adaptations.

EXTENSION ACTIVITY Group students by the home planet of their creatures. Have them compare their alien adaptations. What do the creatures from one planet have in common? The aliens can then be grouped with their planets on the From the Sun wall model.

Sun Strength (Science, Math)

Just how powerful is the Sun? Well, even though it's 93 million miles away, we can be burned by it! Everyone can feel the difference between being in the shade and out in the sun, but measuring the temperature in different sunlight conditions is a good way for students to add numbers to that difference. (The reproducible on page

25 lists materials and detailed directions.) This activity can be done in large or small groups, depending on how many thermometers you have—each group needs three. It can be done outside or inside, wherever you get direct sunlight. Pick a sunny day for best results. And if you'll be doing it inside, schedule the experiment for a time when your windows get direct sunlight.

MANAGEMENT TIPS First photocopy page 25 for each group of students. Explain that *Very sunny* is full, direct sunlight. *Kind of shady* is diffused sunlight, maybe under a tree or through a sheer curtain. *Totally shady* means the sunlight is blocked, for example, under an overhang next to an outside wall or across the room from a window. Each group places their thermometer in an appropriate spot for each category and then goes back after a half hour to record the temperature. Graphing the temperature on the drawn thermometers will help students to compare temperatures with other groups. Have all the groups compare what they found for the three categories. The class then draws conclusions about how much stronger the Sun is in and out of the shade.

EXTENSION ACTIVITY Another way to see the Sun's power is by watching how things fade—like colored construction paper. You'll need a sunny windowsill. Have students arrange objects on a piece of construction paper sitting on a windowsill. They should choose fairly heavy objects like coins, erasers, cups, etc., that won't easily move around. Leave the papers on the windowsill for a week or two. Then have students remove the objects and see that the areas protected from sunlight have kept their color. However, the strong sunlight has broken down the paper's dyes in the exposed areas.

Film Canister Constellations (Science)

Make a mini-planetarium in your classroom! A fun way to learn constellations is to make film-canister models. The reproducible on page 26 has patterns for six constellations, as well as instructions and needed supplies. This activity can be done by students, or yourself, depending on whether students are old enough to work safely with needles and a hammer and nail. The 35mm film canisters that work best are the black kind with softer gray lids. You can use coffee cans instead of film canisters. Just enlarge the pattern discs to fit. If the lids are not opaque enough, paste black construction paper over the outside before poking holes through.

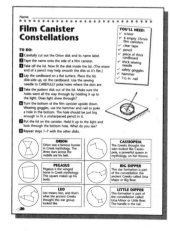

EXTENSION ACTIVITY Students can find additional constellations in books and star charts to make more canister constellations.

How the Stars Came to Be
(Language Arts)

Greeks weren't the only people to see stories in the stars. The reproducible on pages 27–28 is a Native American folktale about how stars came to be. Have students read the legend and discuss it. Ask: Why did the animals go to Great Spirit? According to the folktale, why are some star constellations only half finished? According to the legend, why do coyotes howl at the night sky?

EXTENSION ACTIVITY Invite students to write their own folktale about a constellation or stars in general. Remind them that it doesn't have to be ancient or about animals.

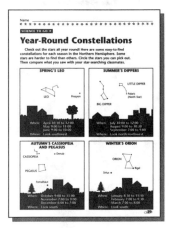

SCIENCE TO GO ➡ Year-Round Constellations (Science)

The reproducible on page 29 is a take-home activity for students. It shows easy-to-find star constellations for each season in North America. Remind students that the farther they can get from street and house lights the better. An adult can help point out the labeled direction in which they should look. Most libraries and bookstores carry star charts of complete constellations. Binoculars are also a help. Some of the individual stars are more difficult to pick out and see than others. Having students circle the stars they see on the reproducible will build their star-searching confidence.

BOOK LINKS

Classroom/Teacher Reference Books

- ◆ *Exploring the Night Sky* by Terrance Dickinson (Camden House, 1987)
- ◆ *Atlas of Stars and Planets* by Ian Ridpath (Facts on File, 1993)

Books for Independent Reading

- ◆ *Planets, Moons and Meteors* by John R. Gustafson (RGA, 1992)

Picture Books

- ◆ *The Magic School Bus Lost in the Solar System* by Joanna Cole (Scholastic, 1990)
- ◆ *My Place In Space* by Robin and Sally Hirst (Orchard Books, 1990)
- ◆ *The Moon* by Seymour Simon (Macmillan, 1984)
- ◆ *What the Moon Is Like* and *The Moon Seems to Change* by Franklyn M. Branley (HarperCollins, 1986, 1987)

Name _____

Create Craters!

The Moon is covered with craters. They are scars from hunks of space rock, called meteors, that hit the Moon. Some craters are big, some small, some round, others crazy-shaped. Why are Moon craters so different? Find out by creating your own Moon craters!

TO DO:

1 Spread newspapers on the floor in front of a wall. Set the pan against the wall on the papers.

2 Place a measuring stick between the pan and the wall. Tape it to the wall if you need to. This setup will let you see the height from which you're dropping the marble.

3 Fill the pan with the salt and flour. Mix them together. Then smooth out the top with an index card.

4 Shake cinnamon on top. This will help the craters show up better. Your moonscape is ready for crashing craters!

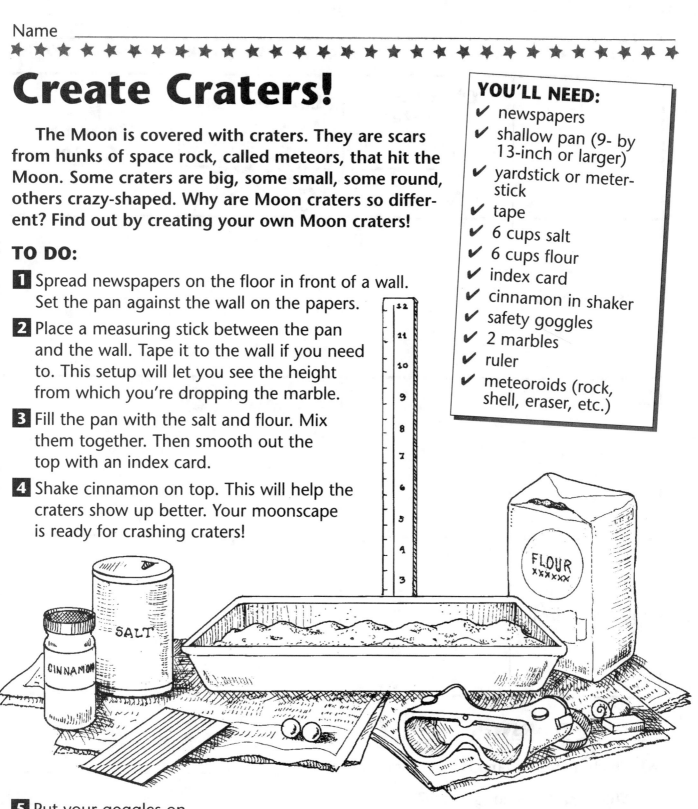

5 Put your goggles on.

6 Hold a marble 12 inches (30 cm) above one side of your moonscape. Drop it.

7 Measure across the crater and the longest ray (looking at the chart helps). Record the information for Meteoroid 1 on the chart.

8 Repeat step 6 holding a marble 36 inches (90 cm) above the other side of your moonscape. Measure and record the information for Meteoroid 2.

9 How are the two craters different? How are they the same?

Name _____

★ ★

	Diameter of Crater 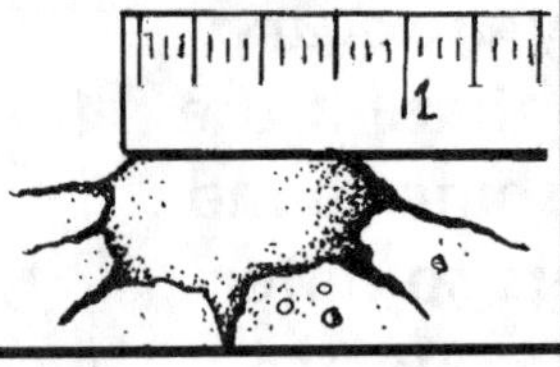	**Longest Ray** 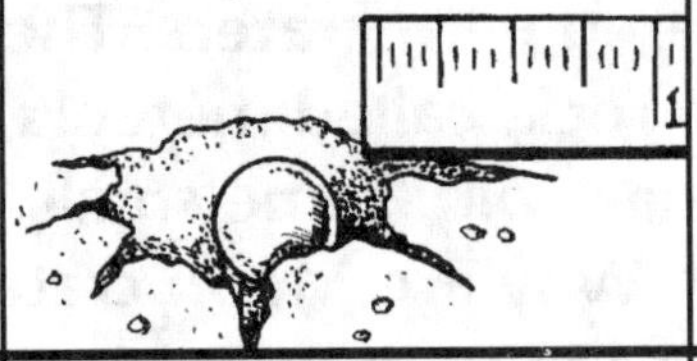	**Draw the Crater**
Meteoroid 1			
Meteoroid 2			
My Meteoroid			

THINK AND ANSWER

1 Which meteoroid made the biggest crater? _____

Which made the longest ray? _____

2 What do you think makes a difference in how a crater is shaped? Why? _____

_____

EXTRA: What else could be a meteoroid? Choose a rock, shell, coin, or other object. Then smooth out the top of your moonscape and re-sprinkle it with cinnamon. Do steps 6–7 again using your meteoroid. What happened? Why?

Planet Patterns

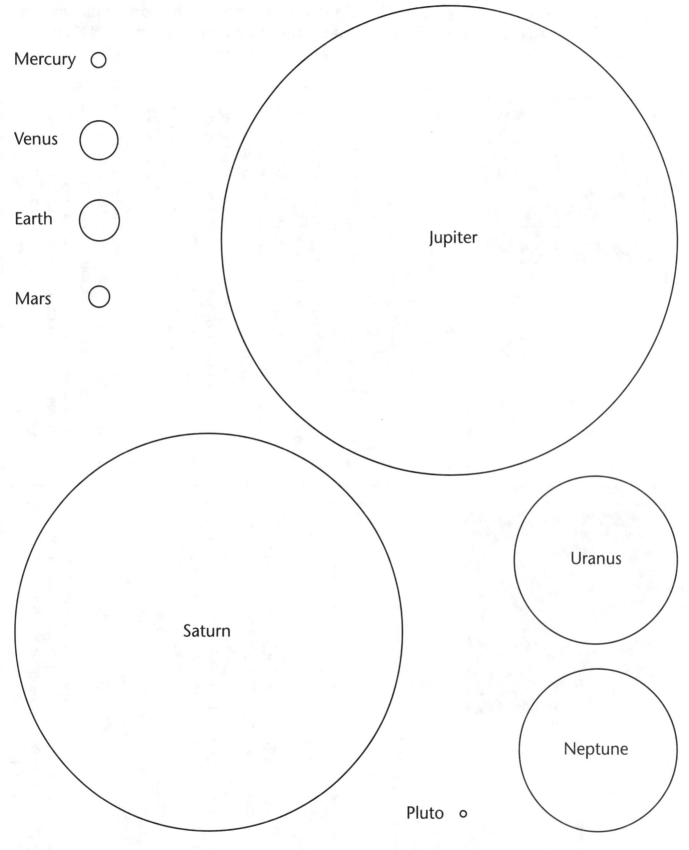

Mercury ○

Venus ○

Earth ○

Mars ○

Jupiter

Saturn

Uranus

Neptune

Pluto ○

SUN
To make a sun, draw a circle with a diameter 9½ times that of Jupiter.

Solar System Fact Cards

The cards on these five pages will help you learn more about our solar system. To make the cards, cut along the solid lines. Then fold along the dashed lines. Tape or paste the front and back of each card together.

MERCURY

Color: gray
Size: 3,031 miles across
From the Sun: 36 million miles
Day (one spin): 59 Earth days
Year (a trip around Sun): 88 Earth days
Orbiting speed: 30 miles per second
Gravity: 85-pound kid would weigh 32 pounds

What it's like: Mercury looks kind of like the Moon. Its gray and rocky land is full of craters. There's hardly any *atmosphere* (air), so the sky is always black. The Sun shines 10 times stronger here than it does on Earth. It gets hot enough to melt lead (800°F) during the day, and cold enough for freezer burn (–275°F) at night.

FAB FACTS

◆ Because Mercury is so close to the Sun, one spin—or "day"—isn't the time from one sunrise to the next, as on Earth. Sunset to sunset takes 176 Earth days!

◆ Look for Mercury close to the horizon in the western sky for an hour after sunset, or in the eastern sky for an hour before sunrise.

◆ Quick-orbiting Mercury was named after the speedy messenger of the Roman gods.

SUN

Color: orange
Size: 865,000 miles across
Day (one spin): 25 Earth days, 9 hours

What it's like: Hot! 11,000°F on the surface. The dark sunspots are a bit cooler—only 7,200°F! Giant storms, called solar flares, spit out hot gas at more than a million miles per hour.

FAB FACTS

◆ The Northern Lights are streaks of glowing colors in the night sky. They are caused by electrically charged particles sent out by the Sun that interact with Earth's upper atmosphere.

◆ A solar eclipse happens when the Moon gets between the Sun and the Earth. Our view of the Sun is then blocked.

◆ NEVER look right at the Sun, even with sunglasses on. It can hurt your eyes.

Solar System Fact Cards

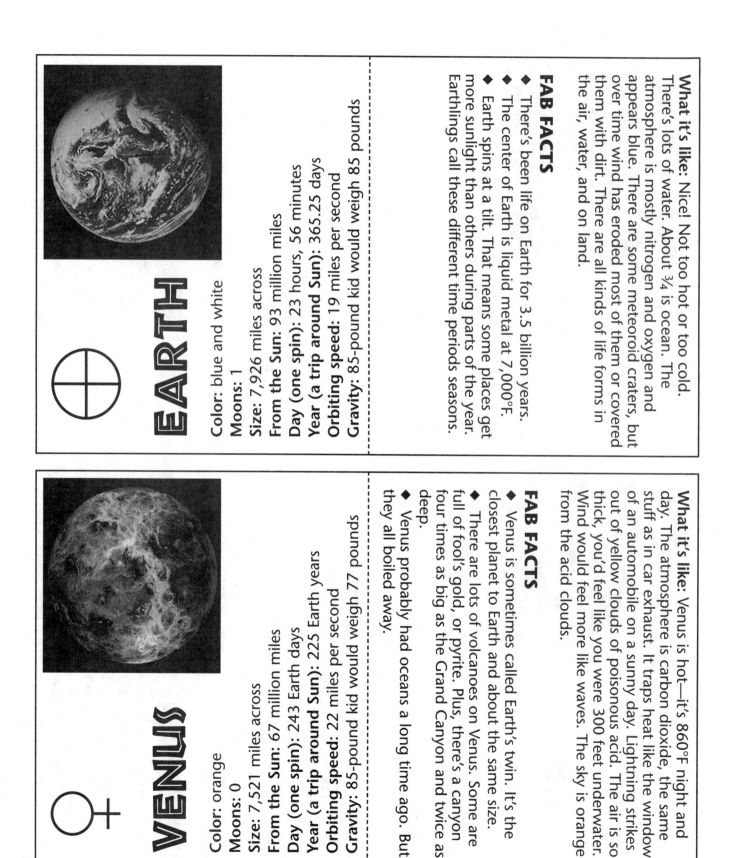

EARTH

Color: blue and white
Moons: 1
Size: 7,926 miles across
From the Sun: 93 million miles
Day (one spin): 23 hours, 56 minutes
Year (a trip around Sun): 365.25 days
Orbiting speed: 19 miles per second
Gravity: 85-pound kid would weigh 85 pounds

What it's like: Nice! Not too hot or too cold. There's lots of water. About ¾ is ocean. The atmosphere is mostly nitrogen and oxygen and appears blue. There are some meteoroid craters, but over time wind has eroded most of them or covered them with dirt. There are all kinds of life forms in the air, water, and on land.

FAB FACTS

◆ There's been life on Earth for 3.5 billion years.
◆ The center of Earth is liquid metal at 7,000°F.
◆ Earth spins at a tilt. That means some places get more sunlight than others during parts of the year. Earthlings call these different time periods seasons.

VENUS

Color: orange
Moons: 0
Size: 7,521 miles across
From the Sun: 67 million miles
Day (one spin): 243 Earth days
Year (a trip around Sun): 225 Earth years
Orbiting speed: 22 miles per second
Gravity: 85-pound kid would weigh 77 pounds

What it's like: Venus is hot—it's 860°F night and day. The atmosphere is carbon dioxide, the same stuff as in car exhaust. It traps heat like the window of an automobile on a sunny day. Lightning strikes out of yellow clouds of poisonous acid. The air is so thick, you'd feel like you were 300 feet underwater. Wind would feel more like waves. The sky is orange from the acid clouds.

FAB FACTS

◆ Venus is sometimes called Earth's twin. It's the closest planet to Earth and about the same size.
◆ There are lots of volcanoes on Venus. Some are full of fool's gold, or pyrite. Plus, there's a canyon four times as big as the Grand Canyon and twice as deep.
◆ Venus probably had oceans a long time ago. But they all boiled away.

Solar System Fact Cards

JUPITER

Color: orange & striped
Moons: 16
Size: 88,849 miles across
From the Sun: 484 million miles
Day (one spin): 9 hours, 55 minutes
Year (a trip around Sun): 11.9 Earth years
Orbiting speed: 8 miles per second
Gravity: 85-pound kid would weigh 216 pounds

What it's like: Bigger than 1,000 Earths! All the gas giant planets (Saturn, Jupiter, Uranus, and Neptune) are like bags of gas with liquid in the middle. There's no solid ground at all. Jupiter's atmosphere consists of hydrogen and helium. Clouds of different-colored gases help give Jupiter its striped look. Below is a slushy ocean of hotter-than-boiling hydrogen.

FAB FACTS
◆ Spaceships will never land on Jupiter—there's no land! Plus, the pressure of the thick gases would crush them.

◆ Jupiter's Great Red Spot is a permanent hurricane the size of three Earths.

◆ Jupiter's moon, Io, has active volcanoes and a frozen surface.

MARS

Color: red
Moons: 2
Size: 4,222 miles across
From the Sun: 142 million miles
Day (one spin): 24 hours, 37 minutes
Year (a trip around Sun): 687 Earth days
Orbiting speed: 15 miles per second
Gravity: 85-pound kid would weigh 32 pounds

What it's like: Mars is a cold desert. Daytime temperatures are rarely above freezing. At night it gets down to –90°F. The very thin atmosphere is mostly carbon dioxide (what we breathe out). There are seasons on Mars—the planet is tilted, like Earth. Winter brings carbon-dioxide frost. Summer means planet-wide dust storms. The red dust in the air makes the sky pink. No proof of life—past or present—has been found on Mars.

FAB FACTS
◆ The two moons of Mars are only 9.3 and 16 miles across. They are shaped like potatoes! They probably used to be asteroids.

◆ Mars has a huge volcano, Olympus Mons. It's three times the size of Mount Everest.

◆ There's no liquid water on Mars now. But maybe there used to be. Some channels, called "Martian canals," might be dried riverbeds.

Solar System Fact Cards

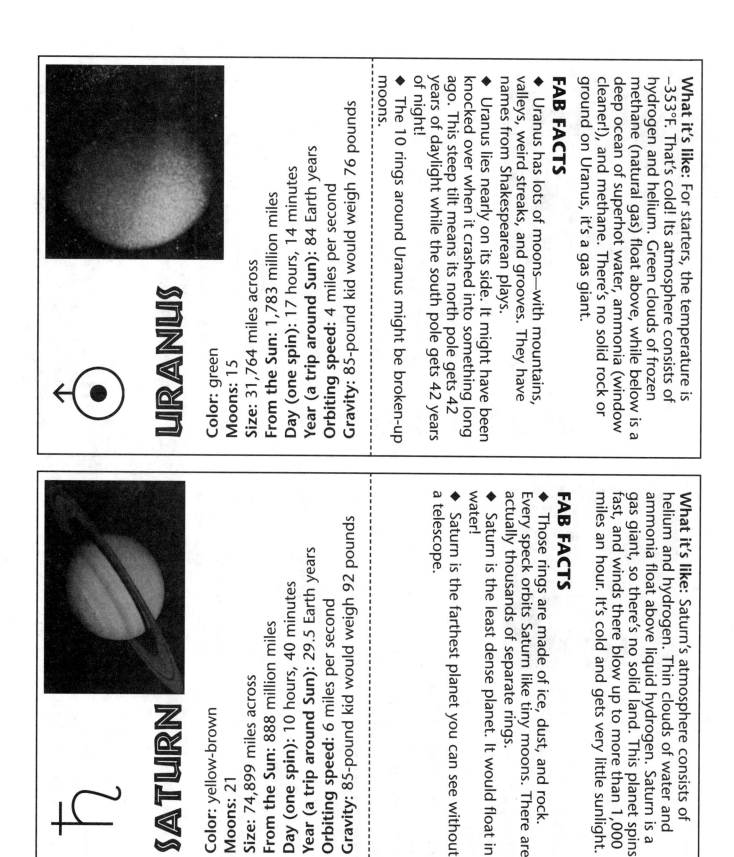

URANUS

Color: green
Moons: 15
Size: 31,764 miles across
From the Sun: 1,783 million miles
Day (one spin): 17 hours, 14 minutes
Year (a trip around Sun): 84 Earth years
Orbiting speed: 4 miles per second
Gravity: 85-pound kid would weigh 76 pounds

What it's like: For starters, the temperature is –353°F. That's cold! Its atmosphere consists of hydrogen and helium. Green clouds of frozen methane (natural gas) float above, while below is a deep ocean of superhot water, ammonia (window cleaner!), and methane. There's no solid rock or ground on Uranus, it's a gas giant.

FAB FACTS

◆ Uranus has lots of moons—with mountains, valleys, weird streaks, and grooves. They have names from Shakespearean plays.

◆ Uranus lies nearly on its side. It might have been knocked over when it crashed into something long ago. This steep tilt means its north pole gets 42 years of daylight while the south pole gets 42 years of night!

◆ The 10 rings around Uranus might be broken-up moons.

SATURN

Color: yellow-brown
Moons: 21
Size: 74,899 miles across
From the Sun: 888 million miles
Day (one spin): 10 hours, 40 minutes
Year (a trip around Sun): 29.5 Earth years
Orbiting speed: 6 miles per second
Gravity: 85-pound kid would weigh 92 pounds

What it's like: Saturn's atmosphere consists of helium and hydrogen. Thin clouds of water and ammonia float above liquid hydrogen. Saturn is a gas giant, so there's no solid land. This planet spins fast, and winds there blow up to more than 1,000 miles an hour. It's cold and gets very little sunlight.

FAB FACTS

◆ Those rings are made of ice, dust, and rock. Every speck orbits Saturn like tiny moons. There are actually thousands of separate rings.

◆ Saturn is the least dense planet. It would float in water!

◆ Saturn is the farthest planet you can see without a telescope.

PLUTO

Color: yellow
Moons: 1
Size: 1,420 miles across
From the Sun: 3,596 million miles
Day (one spin): 6 Earth days, 9 hours
Year (a trip around Sun): 248 Earth years
Orbiting speed: 3 miles per second
Gravity: 85-pound kid would weigh 5 pounds

What it's like: Cold, dark, and frozen. But there's no frozen water, only frozen gases, mostly methane (natural gas). The rocks below these gases are glassy, like sand. The Sun looks merely like a bright star in the always-dark sky.

FAB FACTS

◆ Pluto is smaller than Earth's moon.
◆ Some scientists think that Pluto used to be a moon of Neptune. Maybe it escaped Neptune's gravity and started its own orbit around the Sun.
◆ You'd never live long enough to reach your first birthday on Pluto—the year is too long!

NEPTUNE

Color: greenish blue
Moons: 8
Size: 30,776 miles across
From the Sun: 2,797 million miles
Day (one spin): 16 hours, 7 minutes
Year (a trip around Sun): 164.8 Earth years
Orbiting speed: 3.2 miles per second
Gravity: 85-pound kid would weigh 98 pounds

What it's like: It's cold, about −360°F. The atmosphere is full of hydrogen and helium gases (as in a balloon). Thin, wispy clouds of methane (natural gas) really move. The wind blows at 700 miles per hour! Like all the gas giants (Saturn, Jupiter, Uranus, and Neptune), there's no solid rock or ground—just gas and liquid.

FAB FACTS

◆ Neptune has five thin rings.
◆ Neptune is the farthest planet from the Sun—until 1999. At that point, Pluto becomes the farthest. That's because Pluto's and Neptune's orbits overlap a bit.
◆ The Great Dark Spot on Neptune is a huge storm the size of Earth.

★ ★

Sun Strength: How Hot Is It?

YOU'LL NEED:
- ✔ 3 thermometers
- ✔ masking tape
- ✔ pen or pencil
- ✔ watch

Just how much difference does shade make? Find out by measuring temperatures and filling in the chart!

TO DO:

1 Mark your three thermometers with a masking-tape label. Write your group name on the tape.

2 Find three spots to leave the thermometers: one that's **Very sunny,** one that's **Kind of shady,** and one that's **Totally shady.**

3 After you find a **Very sunny** spot and place a thermometer down, write the Start time on the **Very sunny** chart thermometer below. Do the same when you find a **Kind of shady** spot and a **Totally shady** spot.

4 Leave the thermometers in the spots for a half an hour.

5 After a half an hour, record the End times and the temperatures on the thermometers below.

Very sunny	**Kind of shady**	**Totally shady**
Start time: _____ End time: _____	Start time: _____ End time: _____	Start time: _____ End time: _____

6 Where was it hottest? _____

7 Where was it coolest? _____

8 What's the temperature difference between the coolest and hottest? _____

EXTRA: If your thermometer used °F, change it to °C. Or if you recorded the temperature in °C, change it to °F. (Hint: Use the paper thermometer.)

25

★ ★

Film Canister Constellations

TO DO:

1 Carefully cut out the Orion disk and its information label.

2 Tape the information label onto the side of a film canister.

3 Take off the lid. Now fit the disk inside the lid. (The eraser end of a pencil may help smooth the disk so it's flat.)

4 Place the cardboard on a flat surface. Place the lid, disk-side up, on the cardboard. Use the sewing needle to CAREFULLY poke holes where the dots are.

5 Take the pattern disk out of the lid. Make sure the holes went all the way through by holding it up to the light. Does light show through?

6 Turn the film canister upside down. Wearing goggles, use the hammer and nail to poke a hole in the bottom. The hole should be just big enough to fit an unsharpened pencil in it.

7 Put the lid on the canister. Hold it up to the light and look through the bottom hole. What do you see?

8 Repeat steps 1–7 with the other disks.

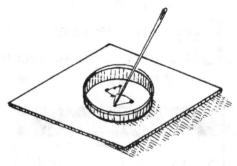

YOU'LL NEED:
- ✔ scissors
- ✔ 6 empty 35mm film canisters
- ✔ clear tape
- ✔ pencil
- ✔ piece of thick cardboard
- ✔ thick sewing needle
- ✔ safety goggles
- ✔ hammer
- ✔ 1½ in. nail

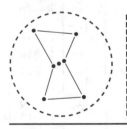

ORION
Orion was a famous hunter in Greek mythology. The three stars across the middle are his belt.

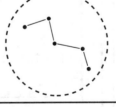

CASSIOPEIA
The Greeks thought the stars looked like Cassiopeia, a powerful queen in mythology, on her throne.

PEGASUS
Pegasus is the winged horse in Greek mythology. This square makes up his body.

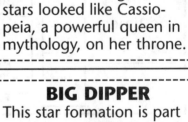

BIG DIPPER
This star formation is part of the constellation the ancient Greeks called Ursa Major or Big Bear.

LEO
Leo means "lion," and that's what the ancient Greeks thought this star group looked like.

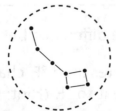

LITTLE DIPPER
This formation is part of the constellation called Ursa Minor or Little Bear. The handle is the tail.

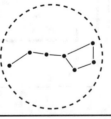

How the Stars Came to Be

A Native American folktale

Long, long ago, there were no stars in the sky. The sun shone in the daytime sky. Often, the moon's light lit up the nighttime sky. But other times, when the moon did not shine, the sky was black as could be. On these dark nights, many of the animals were frightened. Sometimes it was so dark that they could not see to find their way home.

"Good morning, Hare," said Crow. "How are you?"

"I'm happy to be alive, friend Crow," answered Hare. "Last night it was so dark that I couldn't find my burrow."

"I know just what you mean. When the moon doesn't shine, I often crash into that big pine tree near my nest," said Crow. "I wonder if the Great Spirit could help us."

"Let's get Eagle to ask," said Hare.

After Eagle heard about the problem, he flew up into the sky to the Great Spirit.

"Oh, Great Spirit. Hear our plea," said Eagle. "On nights when there is no moon in the sky, we are frightened. The small animals cannot find their way home. Please help us."

Great Spirit said, "Ask all the animals to go down to the river and pick up as many stones as they can carry. Tell them to look for little stones with sharp, pointed edges." Great Spirit showed the animals what to do. He carefully placed a stone high up in the sky. All at once it began to sparkle and glitter.

"Look at that little light up in the sky," said Bear. "What is it?"

"It is called a star, friend Bear," said Great Spirit.

As the animals watched, the star grew brighter.

"I call this the home star," Great Spirit told them. "Look for this star on a dark night, and it will help you find your way home." Then Great Spirit carefully placed other stars in the sky.

"Look, everyone!" exclaimed Crow. "The Great Spirit has made a picture in the sky. The stars make the outline of Brother Badger!"

"That is right," said Great Spirit. "Now, because tonight is a magic night, I will let all of the animals walk off Earth into the sky to make their own star pictures. Take your stones with you. But remember, you must be finished by sunrise!"

All of the animals climbed up into the sky. Each of them chose the perfect spot

to make a star picture. But lazy Coyote was the last animal to go. Just as he was about to head off into the sky, the Great Spirit stopped him.

"Coyote," said Great Spirit. "Some of the animals are too small to carry enough stones to finish their pictures. I want you to take this extra sack of stones. Carry it with you so you can give them a few stones if they run out."

Coyote took the stones, but he did not want to do what the Great Spirit had asked. The bag was heavy.

"I don't see why the Great Spirit always asks me to do the extra work," grumbled Coyote to himself. The farther he walked, the heavier the bag became. Suddenly Coyote stopped. There are more than enough stones in this bag, thought Coyote. No one will know if I throw some of them away.

And that's exactly what Coyote did. He reached in the bag and threw a pawful of stones up into the sky! He did it again and again. And as he threw the stones, they turned into stars and began to twinkle and glow.

Meanwhile, all the other animals were carefully placing their stones in the sky. Soon, however, some of them began to run out of stones to make their pictures.

"Coyote, where are you?" called Bear. "I need a few more stones to finish my picture."

Crow flew all through the sky in search of Coyote. Just as the sun was about to come up, he came upon sleeping Coyote. Beside him lay the empty sack that had been filled with extra stones! By this time, the sun was peeking over the distant hills. It was time for all of the animals to return to Earth. Some of the animals had enough stones and were able to finish their pictures, which is why their star pictures look complete. Other animals did not have enough stones, which is why their star pictures look only half finished.

But lazy Coyote never got around to making a star picture at all. That is why coyotes even to this day look up into the night sky and howl. For when they see all the other animal pictures and all the wasted stars, they think of what a beautiful picture Coyote might have made. Who can blame them for crying?

SCIENCE TO GO ➡

Year-Round Constellations

Check out the stars all year round! Here are some easy-to-find constellations for each season in the Northern Hemisphere. Some stars are harder to find than others. Circle the stars you can pick out. Then compare what you saw with your star-searching classmates.

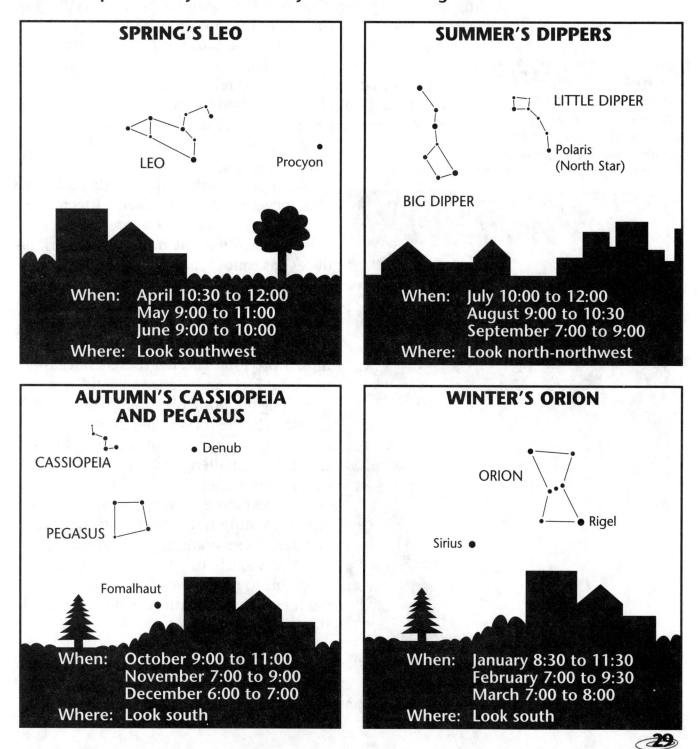

SPRING'S LEO

LEO   Procyon

When: April 10:30 to 12:00
        May 9:00 to 11:00
        June 9:00 to 10:00
Where: Look southwest

SUMMER'S DIPPERS

LITTLE DIPPER

Polaris
(North Star)

BIG DIPPER

When: July 10:00 to 12:00
        August 9:00 to 10:30
        September 7:00 to 9:00
Where: Look north-northwest

**AUTUMN'S CASSIOPEIA
AND PEGASUS**

CASSIOPEIA   • Denub

PEGASUS

Fomalhaut

When: October 9:00 to 11:00
        November 7:00 to 9:00
        December 6:00 to 7:00
Where: Look south

WINTER'S ORION

ORION

• Rigel

Sirius •

When: January 8:30 to 11:30
        February 7:00 to 9:30
        March 7:00 to 8:00
Where: Look south

CHAPTER 2

THE JOURNEY TO SPACE

Rocket Science: Gravity, Friction

Getting to space means overcoming Earth's gravitational pull and escaping the atmosphere. *Gravity* is the force that pulls everything—people, rocks, water, and the air we breathe—toward Earth. So the first step to exploring space is to build something that can escape Earth's grasp—a rocket. Rockets are an old idea: Anything that propels itself by releasing a gas is a rocket. For example, letting go of an inflated balloon is an example of a rocket! Rockets are examples of *Newton's third law of motion:* For every action (the escaping air) there is an equal and opposite reaction (the balloon moving forward).

> **FAST FACT**
>
> Gunpowder rockets were probably first used by the Chinese after they invented gunpowder 1,000 years ago.

A simple Fourth of July bottle rocket has all a rocket needs. It has fuel, a firecracker, and a simple guidance system (the stick). When it's ignited, the burning powder produces gas, smoke, and fire, which escape out the open end, producing a thrust and propelling the rocket in the opposite direction, in this case up. The stick keeps the rocket headed in a single direction as it flies. More sophisticated rockets have more powerful fuels and electronic guidance systems, but the principles are the same. Of course, a bottle rocket doesn't go high enough to clear the atmosphere and enter space. That challenge was met first by developing rockets that had stabilizing fins and burned more powerful liquid fuel, and later by adding stages to rockets. Each rocket stage is a separate engine and fuel tank. The first stage boosts the rocket up, then drops off to reduce weight. Later stages propel it ever higher, with new power as each stage ignites.

Space shuttle Discovery

A rocket with enough power and thrust to make it out into space doesn't do anybody much good if it falls apart on the way—or after it gets there. Building a craft that can withstand the heat, pressure changes, and friction of leaving the atmosphere and entering space is a tough task. The cone shape of rockets—as well as of jets—makes them more aerodynamic. The cone tip literally "cuts" through the air, forcing the air to flow along the rocket's sides instead of pushing against them. Exterior surfaces of spacecraft are smooth to cut down on the friction between the air and surface material. Friction causes things to heat up, as when you warm your hands by quickly rubbing them together. Heat from friction is especially fierce upon reentry. On early missions, NASA used a heat shield made of ceramic material to keep spacecraft from burning up on re-entry. Once the temperature exceeded a particular point, fragments of the shield would break off. In this way, the inside of the vehicle remained cool. The only problem with the system was that the heat shield was damaged and could not be reused. Today, the space shuttle is covered with protective tiles. The tiles absorb the heat, keeping the craft itself cool. Parts of the space shuttle heat up to 2,300°F as it hurtles back toward Earth. The shuttle's high-tech tiles are made of a special sand. You could actually hold a red-hot tile in your hand because its outer edges would already have cooled by the time you picked it up!

Mercury capsule atop an Atlas rocket

Space Milestones

When the Soviet Union launched the first artificial satellite, *Sputnik,* into Earth's orbit on an R-7 rocket in 1957, the space race had begun. The Soviet Union's superior rockets gave them an early lead. The Soviets sent the first Moon probe and the first human into space. But the U.S. was never far behind, and the *Apollo* missions leading up to the first human Moon landing in 1969 were a sure victory as far as the international community was concerned. The Soviets led the way with space stations, sending up the first of many in 1971. The U.S. launched its only space station, *Skylab,* two years later. The U.S. space shuttle, the world's first reusable spacecraft, made its maiden voyage in 1981. Meanwhile, space has become less the sole domain of the old cold warriors. Today, both the European Space Agency and Japan launch satellites and probes, and they are working on plans for their own shuttles and space stations. China, India, Israel, Australia, and a growing number of other countries launch communication satellites with their own rockets. Nowadays, international cooperation seems to be the norm when big space projects are being planned. Governments welcome the sharing of expertise and cost.

The following space milestones chronicle the triumphs and tragedies of the struggle to explore outer space.

1926 U.S. scientist Robert H. Goddard launches the world's first liquid-fuel rocket.

1949 The first rocket to make it to outer space is launched from New Mexico February 24.

1957 The world's first satellite, *Sputnik,* is launched by the Soviet Union October 4.

1957 Laika, the Russian dog, is the first animal in space November 3.

1958 *Explorer 1,* the U.S. satellite equivalent of *Sputnik,* orbits Earth January 31.

1958 The U.S. National Aeronautics and Space Administration (NASA) is formed October 1.

Far side of the Moon

1959 First U.S. astronauts, the *Mercury 7,* are chosen April 27.

1959 First probe to hit the Moon, *Luna 2,* is launched by the Soviet Union September 12. *Luna 3* is launched October 4. It circles the Moon, radioing back the first pictures of the Moon's far side.

FAST FACT

When U.S. lunar probes orbited the Moon photographing its surface, surprising irregularities in the Moon's surface gravity were found. If these gravity "bumps" had not been taken into account, the Apollo missions probably wouldn't have succeeded.

1961 First person to travel in space, Soviet Yuri Gagarin, orbits Earth April 12.

1961 Alan B. Shepard Jr. is the first U.S. astronaut in space May 5.

1962 John Glenn is the first U.S. astronaut to orbit Earth February 20.

1963 Soviet Valentina Tereshkova is the first woman in space June 16. She orbits Earth 45 times.

1965 Soviet Alexei Leonov takes the first space walk using a 10-foot tether March 18.

1966 First docking of two space vehicles in space. U.S. *Gemini 8* meets an orbiting U.S. *Agena* rocket March 16.

1967 U.S. astronauts Gus Grissom, Edward White, and Roger Chaffee are killed when their *Apollo* capsule catches fire during a countdown simulation.

1968 U.S. *Apollo 8* astronauts are the first humans to orbit another celestial body—the Moon, and see its far side. Launch December 21.

Gemini astronaut, June 1965

1969 U.S. *Apollo 11* astronauts Neil Armstrong and Edwin E. "Buzz" Aldrin Jr. are the first humans to walk on the Moon July 20.

1969–72 *Apollo* missions *12, 14, 15, 16,* and *17* land more U.S. astronauts on the Moon. Last humans on the Moon December 11, 1972.

1970 *Apollo 13*'s ill-fated mission was launched on April 11. Six harrowing days later—after an oxygen tank explosion, crippled life support and guidance systems, and the cancellation of their Moon landing—they manage to return safely to Earth.

Apollo *on the Moon*

1971 Soviet Union launches first space station, *Salyut 1,* April 19. Three cosmonauts spend 23 days on the station but die when their capsule leaks air during reentry June 30.

1973 First U.S. Space Station, *Skylab,* is launched May 14. Three astronauts stay on the station 28 days.

1975 Soviet Union launches *Venera 9,* the first probe to photograph the surface of Venus, June 8.

1975 First joint American-Soviet space mission. On July 17, an *Apollo* spacecraft meets and docks with a Soviet *Soyuz* craft. Three astronauts and two cosmonauts conduct experiments for two days.

1975 *Viking 1* probe, first spacecraft to land on Mars, is launched August 20.

1977 *Voyager 2* probe is launched by the U.S. August 20. It photographed Jupiter, Saturn, Neptune, and Uranus before leaving the solar system.

1981 World's first reusable spacecraft with a crew, the U.S. space shuttle *Columbia,* is launched April 12.

1983 Sally Ride is the first American woman in space June 18, 20 years after Valentina Tereshkova.

1983 Guion Bluford is the first U.S. African-American in space August 30.

FAST FACT

The space shuttles are named after famous oceangoing ships.

1984 Marc Garneau is the first Canadian in space October 5.

1986 U.S. space shuttle *Challenger* explodes on liftoff, killing all seven crew members.

1990 *Hubble,* the world's largest space telescope, is put into orbit by U.S. space shuttle *Discovery* April 25.

1992 Mae C. Jemison is the first African-American woman in space September 12.

1995 Physician cosmonaut Valery Polyakov, 52, completes a record 437 days in space on board the Russian space station *Mir.*

Space Probes

While sending people into space is captivating and important, astronaut missions haven't gotten very far away from Earth. Space probes, on the other hand, have traversed the entire solar system. Much of what we know about the Moon, Sun, planets, comets, asteroids, and general space conditions we've learned from space probes. Many of these space workhorses—no bigger than a car or two—have been collecting and transmitting information for more than 20 years. Note: Space probes are usually built and launched in numbered series, such as the 12 *Mariner* probes: *Mariner 1–Mariner 12*. Some individual probes fail and some become famous.

Without the lunar probes, it's likely that the *Apollo* missions would have failed—or not happened at all. The Soviet *Luna* probes orbited the Moon and gave the world its first look at the other side of the Moon in 1959. The seven U.S. *Surveyor* Moon probes landed between 1966 and 1968, sending back closeup video of the Moon as well as testing soil samples for Moon chemistry.

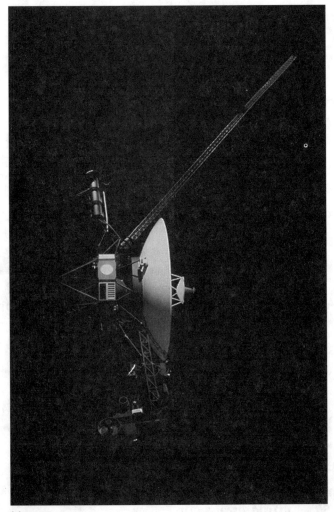

Voyager

Like the lunar probes, interplanetary probes collect and transmit information and photographs, and they pave the way for future missions. The 12 U.S. *Mariner* probes launched in the 1960s and early 1970s flew by Venus, Mars, and Mercury, and many now orbit the Sun. *Mariner 9* orbited Mars; it mapped the entire surface, studied the atmosphere, measured the surface temperature, and sent back more than 7,000 photos—including ones of the Martian moons. The 14 *Pioneer* probes have studied the Sun, Jupiter, Saturn, and Venus. *Pioneer 13* released five landers on Venus, one of which sent back data from the surface. *Pioneer 10* and *11* passed by Jupiter and Saturn in the 1970s. The two *Voyager* probes photographed Jupiter, Saturn, Uranus, and Neptune, along with their many moons and rings. Both *Voyager* probes, as well as *Pioneer 10* and *11*, are now headed out of the solar system toward interstellar space. (See the poster for more about the *Voyager* probes.)

The U.S. Space Shuttle

Today, the space shuttle dominates the U.S. space program. Its ability to be launched like a rocket, orbit and maneuver like a spaceship, and then reenter and land like a jet is remarkable. This reusable spacecraft has a huge cargo bay and can perform a wide variety of scientific, military, and commercial duties on missions lasting weeks.

Shuttle Endeavor

The space shuttle is made up of three main parts: the winged orbiter, the giant external liquid fuel tank, and the two rocket boosters. At launch the orbiter and its fuel and boosters weigh 4.5 million pounds and stand 184 feet tall. An added 65,000 pounds can be carried in the cargo bay. The external fuel tank carries liquid oxygen and hydrogen and the boosters carry solid fuel, which will all be used up within the first 10 minutes of launch. After leaving the atmosphere, the orbiter uses its own engines to maneuver in space.

There are currently four shuttles: *Discovery, Columbia, Atlantis,* and *Endeavor.* (*Challenger* was destroyed in an accident in 1986.) NASA makes six to eight shuttle flights a year. Shuttle missions put satellites into orbit; do repairs in space, as on the Hubble telescope; and perform experiments involving microgravity and how space affects the body. Two pilots and up to six additional crew members fly on each shuttle mission. These are either mission specialists concerned with the operations of the shuttle, or payload specialists, who are experts about the particular payload (cargo) for that mission.

Spacelab is a scientific laboratory that fits inside the cargo bay of the space shuttles. It's connected to the crew compartment by a tunnel. It was built by the European Space Agency. During Spacelab missions, scientists do experiments in manufacturing, astronomy, microgravity, and medicine inside the lab. The first Spacelab mission was in 1983 aboard *Columbia.*

The space shuttle is an important part of Mission to Planet Earth, a NASA program that uses space technology to learn more about our own planet. NASA and others are building a network of Earth-Observing Satellites (EOS) to monitor and map changes in the weather and environmental conditions—for example, effects on the ozone layer. The space shuttle will put some of these satellites into orbit and service them when needed. Space shuttles will also play an important role in building future space stations or Moon bases.

ACTIVITIES

Know the Code! (Science)

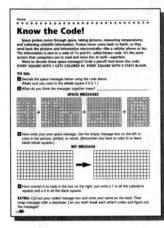

Most computer and digitized (like CDs) information is written in binary code—everything is made up of 0's and 1's, or OFF and ON. Pictures and information transmitted to Earth from space probes and other spacecraft use binary pulses. This is an abstract thing for kids—and adults—to understand, but the reproducible on page 40 helps.

Make a photocopy of the reproducible for each student. Have students decode the messages by shading in all of the boxes with 1's and leaving the boxes with 0's white. What's the message? What do they think it means? (An alien greeting perhaps?) Next, students design a message in the My Message box. Make sure they understand that they have to shade in an entire box or leave it entirely blank. It can be words, a symbol, or a picture. After the message is drawn, have them convert it to code—the shaded boxes are 1's and the blank boxes are 0's.

EXTENSION ACTIVITY Have students create more of their own coded messages with graph paper. Encourage them to use a combination of words and pictures. After encoding them, classmates can exchange them and try to decipher the messages.

Many Milestones (Science, Language Arts)

Space flight and exploration didn't happen overnight. They're the result of the work of many people over most of this century to achieve what was once deemed impossible. The history of space exploration is filled with tragedy, drama, and celebration—there are lots of great stories behind every news headline. Help make the Space Milestones on pages 32–33 more meaningful by having students present reports and make a time line of events.

Assign (or let them choose) a space milestone. Have students research their milestone in the library and write a short report on why they think it was important or interesting. As part of the report, have them create a hanging card that represents their milestone. It could be shaped like the spacecraft or its destination, a silhouette of the person, etc. Make sure they label it with the milestone information and the year. Give them a size (index-card size, for example) so cards will all be proportionate.

Create a time line. You can make the actual line out of construction-paper strips taped to the wall, with a yarn or cord along the wall, or just use colored masking or duct tape. Mark off the years in one-, two-, three-, four-, or five-year intervals, depending on how much space you have (keep in mind that you'll be covering about 70 years). Label the years. Then ask students to tell something about their milestone and to hang it on the time line at the appropriate year. You could have students present their milestones in chronological order.

EXTENSION ACTIVITY There are many more important events in space history than those listed on pages 32–33. Challenge students to find more and add them to the time line. Encyclopedia entries under "space exploration" are great places to find more, as are space almanacs, many of which have time lines of their own.

POSTER: What a Voyager!

The two interplanetary probes launched in 1977, *Voyager 1* and *Voyager 2,* were designed to explore the giant gas planets and their moons. They performed their duties beyond expectations, sending back the best photos yet of Jupiter and Saturn. *Voyager 2* also sent back photos of Uranus and Neptune. Both *Voyager* probes left the solar system in 1989 and continue to traverse interstellar space.

The poster bound in this book's center shows the routes on the *Voyager* probes. Each probe's planet flybys collected an amazing amount of information—a lot of what we know about the gas giants came from these probes. Invite students to choose a particular *Voyager* flyby date marked on the poster and research it. What did we learn from that flyby? Students can present the information to the class.

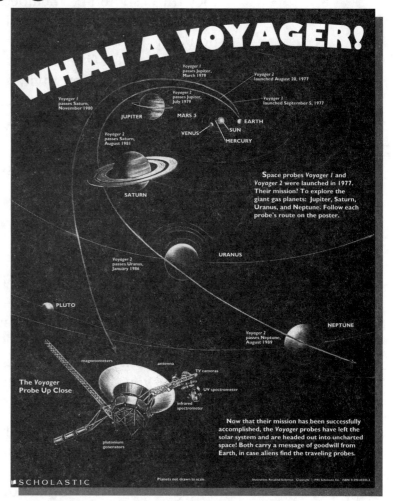

Message in a Space Probe
(Science, Language Arts)

Both *Voyager* space probes are now leaving the solar system. (See the poster.) They will float in open space long after their power sources have been exhausted. What if travelers from another system find one? We hope they'd figure out how to play the gold record attached to the side of the probe. The disk is called "Sounds of Earth" and has two hours of sounds, pictures, and messages from Earth to whoever out there might be listening.

Divide students into groups of three to five. Tell them about the gold disks on the *Voyager* probes. Inform them that new space probes that will explore farther and farther out into space are on scientists' drawing boards. What messages, sounds, pictures, and information do they think should be included with these new probes? How can we tell others about our planet? Have students think about the information that needs to be included: Where Earth is; what it's like here; what kind of life lives here; who humans are exactly; and whether we want to send an open invitation to visit. Ask each group to come up with some ideas for their space probe information disk.

EXTENSION ACTIVITY Have the groups present their ideas to the class and then combine the best of all the groups for display on a wall or bulletin board titled Our Message to the Universe.

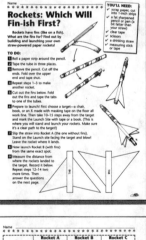

Rockets: Which Will Fin-ish First?
(Science, Math)

Let students discover the stabilizing effect of rocket fins by building and "launching" two rockets—one with fins and one without. Each student will need a copy of the instructions and patterns on pages 41–42. (Materials are listed with the directions on page 41.) Students can also work in pairs with a single set of pages between them. Ask: What do you think rocket fins are for? Predict: How would a rocket with fins fly differently from one without?

MANAGEMENT TIPS You'll need some space for this activity, such as a hallway. Remind students not to shoot their rockets at anyone! When they are inventing their own designs in Extra, help them brainstorm by suggesting they think about how their test rocket would fly with: bent-up fin ends, putting the fins on upside down or on the cone end, heavier fins, smaller fins, etc.

Extension Activity Hold a straw-powered rocket design contest. Winning categories could emphasize both distance and accuracy, such as Farthest Flier and Target Tamer. Make sure everyone uses a same-size "regulation" straw to keep it fair!

SCIENCE TO GO ⟹

My Shuttle Mission
(Science, Critical Thinking)

NASA listens to school kids. The newest shuttle, *Endeavor*, was named by schoolchildren. (*Endeavor* replaced *Challenger* after the accident.) Tomato seeds that were taken into space on a shuttle mission were distributed to classrooms to see how they grew. And there have been a number of NASA student competitions to design space experiments. Let your kids in on the fun by coming up with their own ideas for shuttle missions.

Pass out copies of My Shuttle Mission, page 43. You might go over the items one by one, reminding them: There is air in the crew compartment, but the effects of gravity are different in space so things float. The cargo bay is huge, so they can bring lots of equipment. It takes two pilots to fly the shuttle. Whom do they want for the up to six other crew members? Doctors, satellite experts, veterinarians, astronomers, rocket scientists, engineers?

Extension Activity Encourage students to research whether their missions have flown. They'll be surprised at all the shuttle astronauts have done.

BOOK LINKS

Classroom/Teacher Reference Books

◆ *Rockets: Physical Science Teacher's Guide with Activities* by NASA Education Division (NASA, 1995)

Books for Independent Reading

◆ *The Dream Is Alive* by Barbara Embury (HarperCollins, 1990)

◆ *One Giant Leap* by Mary Ann Fraser (Henry Holt, 1993)

◆ *The Space-shuttle* by George S. Fichter (Franklin Watts, 1990)

Name _____

★ ★

Know the Code!

Space probes zoom through space, taking pictures, measuring temperatures, and collecting scientific information. Probes never come back to Earth, so they send back the pictures and information electronically—like a cellular phone or fax. The information is sent in a code of 1's and 0's, called binary code. It's the same system that computers use to read and store lots of stuff—superfast.

Want to decode these space messages? Grab a pencil! And know the code: EVERY SQUARE WITH 1 GETS COLORED IN. EVERY SQUARE WITH 0 STAYS BLANK.

TO DO:

1 Decode the space messages below using the code above.
(Make sure you color in the **whole** square if it is 1.)

2 What do you think the messages together mean? _____

SPACE MESSAGES

Message 1

0	0	0	0	0	0
1	0	0	1	0	0
1	0	0	1	0	1
1	0	0	1	0	0
1	1	1	1	0	1
1	0	0	1	0	1
1	0	0	1	0	1
1	0	0	1	0	1
0	0	0	0	0	0

+

Message 2

0	0	0	0	0	0	0	0	0	0	0	0	0	0
1	1	1	0	1	0	0	0	0	0	0	0	0	0
0	1	0	0	1	0	0	0	0	0	0	0	0	0
0	1	0	0	0	0	1	0	0	0	0	0	0	0
0	1	0	0	0	0	1	1	1	0	1	1	1	1
0	1	0	0	0	0	1	0	0	1	0	0	1	1
0	1	0	0	0	0	1	0	0	1	0	0	1	1
1	1	1	0	0	0	1	0	0	1	0	0	1	1
0	0	0	0	0	0	0	0	0	0	0	0	0	0

+

Message 3

0	0	0	0	0	0	0	0	0	0	0	0	0
0	0	0	0	0	0	0	0	0	0	0	0	0
0	0	0	0	0	0	0	0	0	0	0	0	0
0	0	0	0	0	0	0	1	0	0	0	0	0
1	1	1	1	1	0	0	1	1	1	1	1	1
1	0	0	0	1	0	0	1	0	0	1	0	1
1	0	0	1	1	0	0	1	0	0	1	0	1
1	1	1	0	1	1	0	1	0	0	1	0	1
0	0	0	0	0	0	0	0	0	0	0	0	0

+

Message 4

0	1	0	0	0	1	0
0	0	1	0	1	0	0
0	1	1	1	1	1	0
0	1	0	1	0	1	0
0	1	1	1	1	1	0
0	1	0	1	0	1	0
0	1	0	0	0	1	0
0	1	1	1	1	1	0
0	0	1	1	1	0	0

3 Now write your own space message. Use the empty message box on the left to color in the picture, symbol, or words. (Remember you have to color in or leave blank whole squares.)

MY MESSAGE

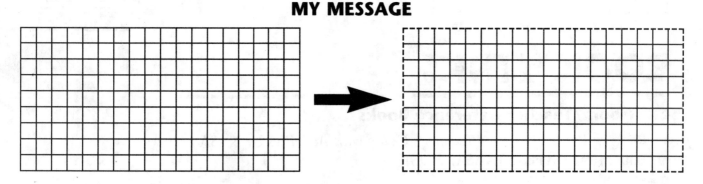

4 Now convert it to code in the box on the right. Just write a 1 in all the colored-in squares and a 0 in all the blank squares.

EXTRA: Cut out your coded message box and write your name on the back. Then swap messages with a classmate. Can you both break each other's codes and figure out the messages?

Name _____

Rockets: Which Will Fin-ish First?

Rockets have fins (like on a fish). What are the fins for? Find out by building and launching your own straw-powered paper rockets!

YOU'LL NEED:
- ✔ scrap paper, cut into 1-inch strips
- ✔ fat sharpened pencil or pen (a bit fatter than your straw)
- ✔ clear tape
- ✔ scissors
- ✔ drinking straw
- ✔ measuring stick or tape

TO DO:

1 Roll a paper strip around the pencil.

2 Tape the tube in three places.

3 Remove the pencil. Cut off the ends. Fold over the upper end and tape shut.

4 Repeat steps 1–3 to make another rocket.

5 Cut out the fins below. Fold out the fins and tape the tabs to one of the tubes.

6 Prepare to launch! First choose a target—a chair, book, or an X made with masking tape on the floor all work fine. Then take 10–15 steps away from the target and mark the Launch Site with tape or a book. (This is where you will stand and launch your rockets. Make sure it's a clear path to the target!)

7 Slip the straw into Rocket A (the one without fins). Stand on the Launch Site facing the target and blow! Leave the rocket where it lands.

8 Now launch Rocket B (with fins) from the same exact spot.

9 Measure the distance from where the rockets landed to the target. Record it. Repeat steps 7–9 two more times. Then answer the questions on the next page.

TAB

TAB

Name _____

★ ★

Launch	Rocket A	Rocket B	Rocket C
First Launch			
Second Launch			
Third Launch			

THINK AND ANSWER:

1 Did Rocket A or B come closer to the target?_____

2 What do you think the fins are for? _____

_____

_____

EXTRA: Use another paper strip to make Rocket C. Attach your own fin design. Then launch it and record the results on the chart. How did it measure up to Rockets A and B?

Name _____

★ ★

My Shuttle Mission

1 Mission Name: _____

2 What mission will do: _____

_____

_____

3 How it will do that: _____

_____

_____

4 Equipment to bring: _____

_____

_____

5 Number of days (no more than 16!): _____

6 Crew: _____ 2 pilots, _____

_____

_____

EXTRA: One of NASA's space-shuttles is always taking off. Watch or read the news to find out how similar a current mission is to yours!

CHAPTER 3

SURVIVING IN SPACE

Getting the Basics

Building spacecraft that could reach outer space was a scientific triumph. And using that technology to take humans into space has been called the greatest achievement of our century. Space is not a natural environment for the human body. There is no air to breathe, temperatures vary from burning hot to freezing cold, pressure changes are severe, and there's no protection from the Sun's harmful radiation. Most of these conditions had to be compensated for before humans could travel in space. Astronauts take their air into space with them; spacecraft have hulls that protect against heat and radiation; and suits or spacecraft are pressurized like jet airplane cabins.

Space shuttle Atlantis

However, gravity is another matter. A spacecraft launched to orbit Earth first speeds up to defy gravity and penetrate the atmosphere. But once it makes it to 200–300 miles above Earth, it slows down. Earth still has a big gravitational pull on anything only a few hundred miles away from it, so gravity starts pulling the spacecraft back down—that is, the craft falls toward Earth. Meanwhile, though, its engines are moving the craft forward, and because the Earth is round, this forward motion actually causes the craft to move away from Earth—much like a thread being pulled off a ball of yarn. What all this moving forward while falling toward Earth means is that the craft orbits—it continually "falls" around Earth in a curved path. This free fall toward Earth that the craft and everyone in it experiences is called weightlessness, or microgravity. It's just like skydivers who can do flips in the air in free fall. It just doesn't seem like falling because they never encounter anything (like the ground) to fall onto.

> ## FAST FACT
> Astronauts aren't really "weightless" in orbit. They are actually in free fall or microgravity.

Microgravity, or weightlessness, can't be compensated for in space with current technology; astronauts have to adapt to it. Everything floats: Nothing stays put unless it's snapped, Velcro-ed, clipped, or strapped down. Most astronauts like being weightless—heavy things are easy to move and floating is fun. There's no need for chairs or mattresses, as the body doesn't ever "rest" (put pressure) on something else. But it turns out microgravity is hard on the human body.

We evolved under the constraints of gravity. To defy gravity by standing up or making a jump shot needs our strong bones and powerful muscles. Bones in space lose minerals such as calcium and weaken; muscles atrophy as with someone who's bedridden; body fluids "settle" in the head, causing a puffy face and sinus congestion; and there's "space sickness," which is kind of like seasickness, with nausea and sometimes vomiting.

Sleep can be somewhat difficult in space. Most astronauts strap themselves into sleeping bags so they don't just float around. Many use eyeshades, as the Sun rises every 90 minutes in an Earth-orbiting craft. Bathroom tasks can be tricky! Bathing on the shuttle's one- or two-week missions is pretty much just a sponge bath with wet towels—water isn't abundant. By the way, water is not carried into space on the shuttle—it's made in space. Fuel cells generate electricity and combine hydrogen and oxygen to make water. Space stations have more permanent shower stalls that vacuum the water away after it is sprayed. Because of microgravity, toilets have footholds, seat belts, and handholds! After sitting on the seat and strapping in, the astronaut turns on an air suction that pulls all the wastes into a storage tank.

Exercise in space is very important. Some astronauts use treadmills or stationary bicycles. But although this keeps the heart and lungs healthy, it doesn't really work on muscles and bones because of microgravity. Scientists are experimenting with "weightlifting" equipment that uses springs or hydraulics to push and pull against. This will curb muscle atrophy. Also, putting stress on bones will help lessen mineral loss. Developing effective exercise regimes is essential if humans are going to spend long periods of time working or traveling in space.

Testing a prototype shower for a space station

Supper in Space

Eating and drinking in space has come a long way since the days of the *Mercury, Gemini,* and *Apollo* missions. John Glenn in his *Mercury* orbital flight squeezed a baby-food-like puree out of a tube for lunch. Later came cubes of meat, fruit, or bread "sealed" with gelatin. Mission control was worried that crumbs would float into and gunk up sensitive instruments. There are problems besides crumbs when it comes to making space food. Because space and weight have to be kept to a minimum, a lot of the food is dehydrated or freeze-dried. It's then reconstituted in individual containers. There are no refrigerators, so all food must be preserved by its packaging and/or processing, or be nonperishable (like nuts).

These days, shuttle astronauts eat fairly normal food, but not in a very normal way. Microgravity means that the table must be set with Velcro strips to anchor the food containers and dining astronauts. Drinks come in closed containers with a straw. Otherwise, the astronauts' morning coffee would float out of their cup. But regular forks and spoons deliver warmed reconstituted chicken teriyaki and scrambled eggs to astronauts' mouths. They must eat slowly, though, to keep the food from flying off the spoon and floating into a wall, neighbor, or piece of equipment. Most food comes in sauce or gravy to help it stick to the utensils. Salt and pepper would become floating grains that might clog instruments or get into eyes and lungs, so astronauts use squeezable liquid salt and pepper sauces instead.

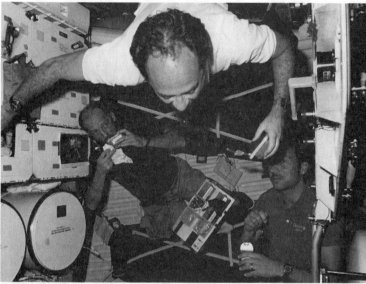
Astronauts train to eat in space.

FAST FACT
Shuttle astronauts take turns as "cook" during mission meals. The "cook" assembles the food packets onto individual trays and heats them up for the crew.

Suit Up!

There's no atmosphere in space, so astronauts take one with them—a spacesuit. In general, spacesuits must be airtight and pressurized, as well as temperature and humidity controlled; protect against heat, radiation, and small flying debris; have a water supply and waste-disposal system; and be flexible enough to allow movement and permit work tasks. That's a tall order, but specific spacesuits need to battle only the particular conditions they'll encounter. The spacesuits the moon walkers wore were very different from what the shuttle astronauts wear on their spacewalks. Those *Apollo* moon-landing suits were one size fits all and made of 17 protective layers including Teflon-coated glass fiber, aluminum-coated plastic, and rubber. The astronauts had to worry about stomping around on moon rocks and possibly damaging their communication equipment. The shuttle astronauts, on the other hand, wear suits that can be adjusted in size for a better fit. Shuttle astronauts also have special reentry suits to keep the pressure changes at bay and in case they need to parachute out in an emergency.

FAST FACT
The first spacesuits were just modified pressure suits that jet pilots wore.

ACTIVITIES

Rubber Bones (Science)

Living in the microgravity of space can cause bones to lose strength-giving minerals, especially calcium. Scientists believe this is because inadequate stress (such as the pulling by muscles and the pounding when walking) is put on the bones. Scientists are therefore trying to include more bone-healthy exercises on shuttle missions, along with special vitamins to solve this problem. Students can see for themselves what happens to bones depleted of calcium in this activity.

MATERIALS

two similar cleaned chicken bones ◆ jar with a lid ◆ white vinegar

DIRECTIONS

1 Place one bone in the jar and pour in enough undiluted vinegar to cover it. Leave the other bone uncovered on a plate.

2 Screw the lid on tightly.

3 After at least a week (two weeks if it's a thick leg bone), take the bone out and dry it off.

4 Have students compare it to the untreated chicken bone.

Ask: What makes bones strong? *(minerals, especially calcium)* How are these two bones different? *(The vinegar-treated bone is rubbery.)* What do you think happened? *(The vinegar removed calcium from the bone, leaving it weak and rubbery.)* How is this like what happens to bones in space?

Astronauts on board the space shuttle Columbia *in 1992*

Preserve It! (Science)

Space food has to last from launch to landing without spoiling and without refrigeration. This means most is canned, dehydrated, vacuum-sealed, freeze-dried, chemically preserved, or irradiated. Let students compare some food preservation methods. In the following activity partners will choose a food, treat it to different preservation methods, and monitor the results over a week.

MATERIALS

fruits and vegetables (carrots, apples, and other not-too-juicy kinds are best) ◆ knives ◆ scrap paper ◆ pencil ◆ means to dry some slices (microwave or cafeteria oven) ◆ self-lock sandwich bags ◆ aluminum foil ◆ fresh-fruit preservative like Stay Fresh ◆ wax paper ◆ masking tape ◆ one copy of page 51 for each pair

DIRECTIONS

1 Have partners choose and slice up their food into four same-size slices.

2 Have each pair put one of their slices on a slip of paper with their names. Gather these up and dry them. Low-oven temperatures for a few hours or about 10 minutes on a low-microwave setting should do it. But make sure they are well dried. (This could be done beforehand and the dried slices handed out to save time.)

3 In the meantime, have students place one of their slices in a plastic bag; wrap another in aluminum foil; and sprinkle the preservative (or dip it in solution—read your product's instructions) on the third and set it on a square of wax paper.

4 Have students tag each slice with its method on masking-tape labels.

5 Ask students to check the slices the next day, after three days, and after a week. (They'll have to open and reclose the foil one.) Have them make observations and drawings on the reproducible's chart. Then have them answer the questions at the page bottom and discuss the answers.

NOTE If you have access to any "higher tech" preserving methods like a sealing machine or canning supplies, just add them to the reproducible's categories.

EXTENSION ACTIVITY Have pairs that experimented on the same food get together and write their recommendations for the best way to preserve that particular food for space flight.

Mission Menu (Science)

Now that students know something about what it takes to feed an astronaut, let them plan a menu for a shuttle mission. Have them keep in mind: There's no refrigerator—but there is an oven to heat the containers; nothing too crumbly or it just ends up floating around; sauces and gravy help the food stick to forks and spoons; everything comes in single-serving containers; and most is canned, dehydrated, or dried. They should remember that astronauts need balanced, healthful meals—and like variety! Have each student plan three meals a day and a snack for a four-day mission (all the astronauts eat the same thing). Each food should say what it is: canned, reconstituted (dehydrated, with hot water added), dried (like fruits, etc.) Here's an example of a dinner:

DAY 1 DINNER
shrimp creole (reconstituted and heated)
potato patty (vacuum-packed, heated)
creamed spinach (reconstituted and heated)
almonds (normal)
vanilla pudding (can)
lemonade (sipping pouch)

Here is a list of some actual space shuttle foods to help students envision the culinary possibilities: beef tips with mushrooms, rice pilaf, Italian vegetables, beef goulash, sweet and sour chicken, green beans, broccoli, strawberries, meatballs with barbecue sauce, potatoes au gratin, chicken teriyaki, rice and chicken, asparagus, almonds, Mexican scrambled eggs, chicken consommé, dried apricots, beef patty, blueberry yogurt, oatmeal, sausage patty, chocolate instant breakfast, tea, orange juice, apple cider, and coffee.

EXTENSION ACTIVITY Astronauts need about 3,000 calories a day. Have your students include portion size and caloric value with the menus to make sure they measure up.

A Suitable Suit (Science, Critical Thinking)

Page 52 shows two current NASA space-shuttle suits: the EMU—(extravehicular mobility unit), and the LES (launch entry suit). The LES is worn inside the shuttle during launch and reentry. The EMU is for working outside the shuttle in open space. Distribute a photocopy to each student and start a discussion on how the two suits are differ-

ent. Have the students answer the questions on the reproducible. *[Possible answers: 1. Both suits have boots, communications assemblies (headsets), gloves, oxygen, helmets, and pressure-resistant covering. 2. The EMU has lights (space is dark), TV camera (so astronauts inside shuttle can see too), caution and warning computer (suit is complicated), drink bag (space walks sometimes last hours), thicker suit (space conditions are harsher), display and control module, and visor. Astronauts inside the shuttle don't need these things. 3. Parachute (in case of need to eject during launch or reentry), life raft, life preserver, and seawater release (in case of crash in ocean), survival gear (in case of crash on landing or takeoff). None of these would help an astronaut in space. 4. The LES has to have lifesaving and survival gear in the event of an accident during landing or takeoff. 5. The EMU has a camera so the astronauts inside the shuttle can see what's going on and perhaps assist. 6. EMU, EMU, LES.]*

EXTENSION ACTIVITY Now that students have connected form with function in two different situations, let their imaginations take off. Have students choose a planet or moon in our solar system and design and draw a spacesuit for exploring that moon's or planet's surface. Their planet fact cards will come in handy.

SCIENCE TO GO ➡ Get a Grip!
(Critical Thinking)

You trade mobility for protection when it comes to spacesuits. The multiple layers of materials add bulk and restrict movement. The activity on page 53 will give your students an idea of what it's like to work in cumbersome spacesuit gloves. Distribute a copy of the page to each student to take home. Encourage students to invite a sibling or parent also to attempt to get a grip.

BOOK LINKS

Classroom/Teacher Reference Books

◆ *U.S. Space Gear: Outfitting the Astronaut* by Lilian D. Kozloski (Smithsonian Institution Press, 1994)

Books for Independent Reading

◆ *Living in Space* by Don Berliner (Lerner, 1993)
◆ *Zero Gravity* by Gloria Skurzynski (Bradbury, 1994)

★ ★

Preserve It!

Our food _____ Today's Date _____

Preserver	after 1 day	after 3 days	after a week
foil			
plastic bag			
dried			
preservative powder			

THINK & ANSWER

1 Which preserver left your food OK to eat after a week? _____

2 Which preserver do you think would be best for space food? Why? _____

_____

_____

Name _____

★ ★

A Suitable Suit

Launch Entry Suit (LES)   **Extravehicular Mobility Unit (EMU)**

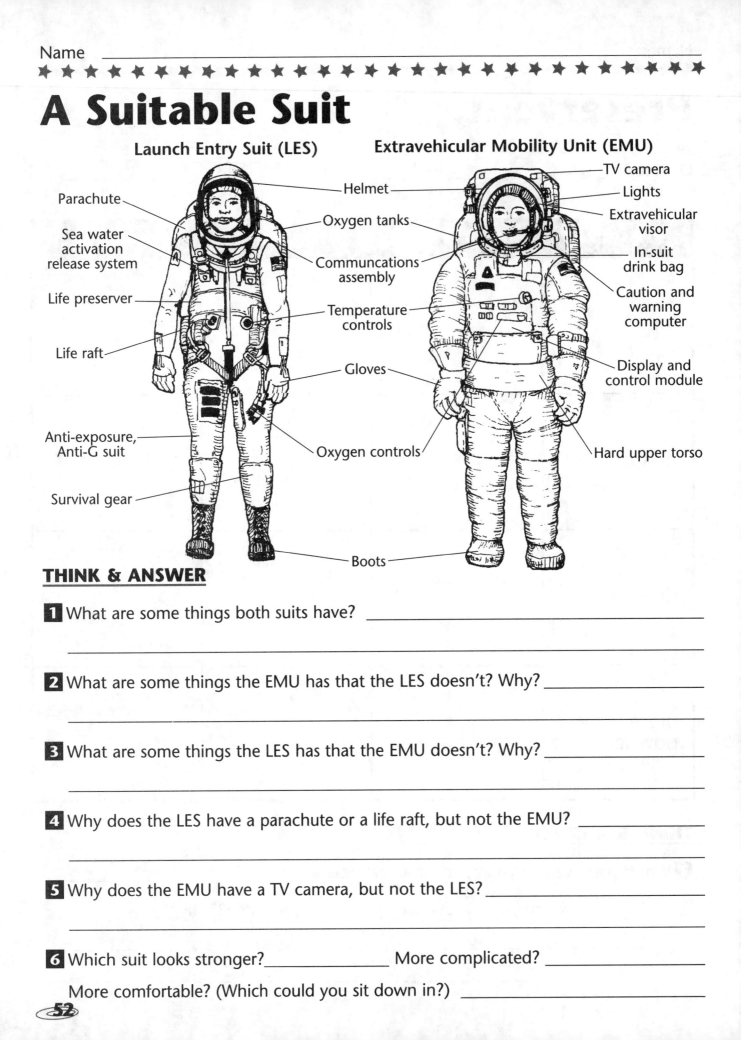

THINK & ANSWER

1 What are some things both suits have? _____

_____

2 What are some things the EMU has that the LES doesn't? Why? _____

_____

3 What are some things the LES has that the EMU doesn't? Why? _____

_____

4 Why does the LES have a parachute or a life raft, but not the EMU? _____

_____

5 Why does the EMU have a TV camera, but not the LES? _____

_____

6 Which suit looks stronger? _____ More complicated? _____

More comfortable? (Which could you sit down in?) _____

★ ★

SCIENCE TO GO ▮▶

Get a Grip!

YOU'LL NEED:
- ✔ adult-size work glove or roomy leather glove
- ✔ cotton balls, facial tissues, or toilet tissue
- ✔ needle and thread
- ✔ toothpicks
- ✔ small building blocks

Astronauts need spacesuits to protect them from the pressure, temperatures, and radiation in space. But the thick heavy suits can make moving around tough. In this activity, you'll find out how hard it must be to "get a grip" with a spacesuit glove on!

TO DO:

1 Stuff the glove with tissue or cotton. Leave enough room for your hand to slide in, though.

2 Suit up! (Put the glove on.)

3 Now try threading a needle, picking up toothpicks, and stacking blocks with the glove on.

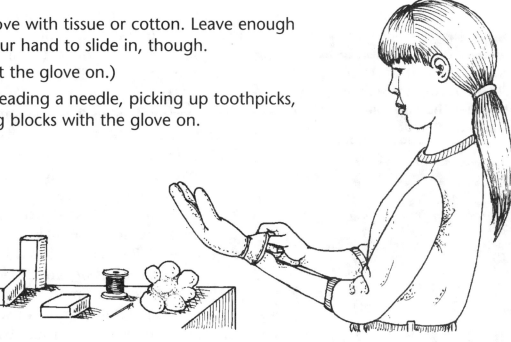

THINK & ANSWER

4 What did the spaceglove feel like? _____

_____

_____

5 What exactly was hard to do with the spaceglove on? _____

_____

_____

6 How could you change the blocks so they'd be easier to stack "in space"? _____

_____

_____

CHAPTER 4

THE ASTRONAUTS

Who Makes It to Space?

Astronauts or cosmonauts are people who work in space. Mostly, they are the men and women of NASA and the former Soviet Union's space programs. But these days, countries besides the U.S. and Russia have space programs and astronauts. The majority of astronauts and cosmonauts are pilots, engineers, doctors, and scientists.

The first U.S. astronauts were chosen in 1959, for the *Mercury 7* program: Walter Schirra, Donald Slayton, John Glenn, Scott Carpenter, Alan Shepard, Gus Grissom, and Gordon Cooper. They were all married men in their thirties with engineering degrees, who had at least 1,500 hours of flying time as military test pilots. In addition, all had to be shorter than 5 feet 11 inches to fit into the small capsule. The original 508 applicants from the military services were X-rayed, tested, baked, frozen, and tossed around in spinning machines to find these seven men with the "right stuff." Between 1959 and 1969, the *Mercury, Gemini, Apollo,* and *Skylab* programs selected a total of 73 men as astronauts—43 of whom actually flew in missions. Civilian test pilots were chosen as astronauts among the second group in 1962. The first civilian scientist astronauts were chosen among the fourth group in 1965.

Astronauts in the space shuttle era were recruited from a wider range of people. In 1978, 35 new space shuttle astronaut candidates, including 6 women, were selected from more than 8,000 applicants. Currently, NASA chooses about 20 astronaut candidates every two years. In general, they are looking for knowledgeable and skilled people who learn fast, are in good health, can keep cool in stressful situations, and work well with others in cramped quarters!

Shuttle astronauts fall into two types: *pilots* and *mission specialists.* Pilot candidates must have a math, science, or engineering bachelor's degree; 1,000 hours of jet flight time, preferably some as a test pilot; pass a rigorous physical-fitness exam; and be between 5 feet 4 inches

> **FAST FACT**
>
> The U.S. Department of Defense also calls the test pilots who fly aircraft higher than 50 miles above Earth astronauts.

Gemini *Astronauts Young, Grissom, Schirra, and Stafford*

and 6 feet 4 inches tall. Mission specialist candidates do experiments, make space walks, and repair and launch satellites and other space equipment. They must have a math, science, or engineering degree plus an advanced degree or at least three years of related work experience; pass a physical-fitness exam; and be between 5 feet and 6 feet 4 inches tall. Sometimes crew members besides pilots and mission specialists fly on shuttle missions. *Payload specialists* conduct experiments related to the particular payload (cargo) of a mission. They often work for that payload's owner, for example, a defense contractor or satellite company. *Space flight participants* have included politicians and schoolteachers. These people aren't in NASA and don't have to be U.S. citizens, but they must pass physical tests and complete space training before launch.

Astronauts Train Tough

Being selected as a space shuttle astronaut candidate is only the beginning. Once candidates arrive at the Johnson Space Center in Houston, Texas, they train long and hard before earning a mission assignment. Training comes in three stages. All candidates must first complete a year of basic training to graduate to active astronaut (not candidate) status. Then they enter a "training pool" of astronauts from which individuals are chosen to crew missions. When an astronaut is assigned to a shuttle mission, he or she starts advanced/flight specific training for a year or so, until that mission actually flies.

Basic training for astronaut candidates includes classes in geology, engineering, astronomy, spacecraft design, and human physiology. Both pilot and mission specialist candidates undergo flight training in T-38 jets. They are exposed to microgravity by working underwater in scuba gear—about the closest thing to microgravity here on Earth. Candidates are given survival training in the event of an emergency water landing or parachute escape. They also receive mission training, in which they learn the layout of the shuttle cockpit and flight-control systems. How well the candidates perform all their basic training tasks determines whether they are accepted as full-fledged astronauts.

An astronaut in training

Making it through basic training and becoming an astronaut doesn't mean you get an assignment to crew a shuttle mission right away. Most astronauts wait and train an average of five more years before flying in space. Some have waited as long as 19 years for their chance to blast off. While waiting, astronauts keep training and learning how to operate new equipment. Many are instrumental in designing

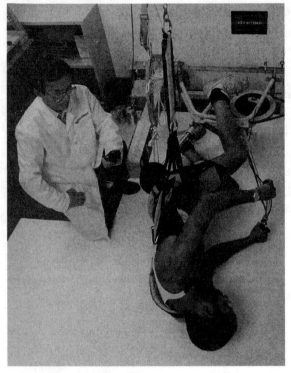

A bicycle is positioned horizontally and the cyclist is suspended to simulate weightlessness.

space equipment that will be used on future missions. Others work with the orbiting astronauts as ground support, relaying needed information. Still others become specialists in jet-pack space walking, operating the shuttle's robotic arm or Spacelab. The more skills astronauts have, the more likely they will be assigned to crew a shuttle mission.

Once astronauts are assigned an actual mission (hooray!), they enter flight-specific or advanced training until the launch date arrives. Every shuttle mission is different. Some missions last only a few days, others more than two weeks. The cargo bay carries everything from a satellite to Spacelab. Therefore, training for a mission concentrates on what will be done—and what problems might come up—for that particular mission. Much of the astronauts' time is spent practicing shuttle operations in simulators. These simulators reproduce conditions of the upcoming missions. Instructors present the crew with emergency problems they must solve. A full-size simulated shuttle model is called a mock-up. Astronauts practice living, working, and checking equipment in cramped quarters during mock-up training. A rookie astronaut might be in advanced training for a year and a half before a mission. But a veteran astronaut may need only six months of training before going back into space.

FAST FACT

Astronaut trainees get a taste of microgravity during so-called vomit comet flights like this one at right. In these flights, where an airplane free falls in an arc like a tossed baseball, causing short intervals of microgravity—and often air sickness.

ACTIVITIES

Amazing Astronauts and Cosmonauts Mini-book
(Science, Language Arts)

Astronauts are amazing people. Introduce students to 10 astronauts and cosmonauts by assembling the mini-book on pages 60–64.

MATERIALS

photocopies of pages 60–64 for each student ◆ tape or paste ◆ construction paper ◆ hole punch ◆ yarn or string

DIRECTIONS

1 Have each student paste or tape page 60 (cosmonauts Gagarin and Polyakov) to a piece of construction paper. The blank side will be the book's cover.

2 Assemble the book's inside pages. Page 61 (astronauts Sullivan and Glenn) is **turned upside down** and pasted or taped to the back of upright page 62 (astronauts Tereshkova and Bluford). Then page 63 (Ride and Armstrong) is **turned upside down** and taped or pasted to the back of upright page 64 (Schmitt and Young). (You could make these as double-sided inverted copies instead.)

page 60 (paste cover to back)

page 62 (paste page 61 to back)

page 64 (paste page 63 to back)

3 Have students punch holes where indicated on each page's fold lines.

4 Have students order the pages correctly. This is a good time to check for problems!

5 Students then fold the pages over and thread a piece of yarn or string through the holes to bind the book together.

EXTENSION ACTIVITY Invite students to decorate their mini-book covers. They could make a collage of pictures of spacecraft, and astronauts, or draw something themselves.

About an Astronaut
(Science, Language Arts)

There are many famous and notable astronauts besides those starring in the Amazing Astronauts and Cosmonauts mini-book. All astronauts and cosmonauts are exceptional people. And behind each name is a story, often of starry childhood dreams, challenges met, obstacles overcome, and driving determination. In short, each holds inspiring lessons for children about reaching personal goals of the highest kind! Let students explore an astronaut's story in this activity.

Each student needs a copy of page 65. Encourage them to choose an astronaut they are interested in. The fact cards are a start and there are many more astronaut names in Space Milestones. The information needed can be found in biographies, encyclopedias, and books about space in the library.

EXTENSION ACTIVITY These reports make good class presentations. If many students have chosen the same astronaut, they can make a presentation as a group.

Why I'd Make a Good Astronaut
(Critical Thinking)

Before being accepted into the NASA astronaut program, the candidate faces a panel of astronauts past and present who ask questions. The panelists know what it takes to be an astronaut. They are also looking for potential crew members they'd be able to work with and trust in life-threatening situations. Candidates have to sell themselves as future astronauts. Have your students do the same—in writing. First, start a classroom discussion about what makes a good astronaut. Learns fast? Cool under pressure? Adventurous? Easygoing? Ask them to think about the things they've done that are similar to what astronauts do during training—swimming, g-force amusement rides, eating camping rations, studying science and math, flying in jets, etc. Then ask each student to write a letter to an astronaut panel saying why he or she would make a good astronaut.

EXTENSION ACTIVITY Have students elect astronaut candidates based on the letters.

Neil Armstrong: To the Moon!
(Language Arts)

Pages 66–70 contain a read-aloud play about the first Moon landing of *Apollo 11* in 1969. Students can take turns reading the dramatic story of how "the world's best pilot," Neil Armstrong, safely landed the lunar module on the Moon.

EXTENSION ACTIVITY Have groups of students write a play about another dramatic space event, like the events of the *Apollo 13* mission.

SCIENCE TO GO ▶ My Training Program
(Personal Health)

Training to be an astronaut includes being physically fit. Astronauts don't have to be Olympic athletes, but they must be fit enough to withstand the stresses of space flight and possible emergency situations. Encourage students to improve their personal fitness with this activity. Make enough copies of page 71 for each student to take one home.

BOOK LINKS

Books for Independent Reading

◆ *John Glenn: Astronaut and Senator* by Michael D. Cole (Enslow, 1993)

◆ *Neil Armstrong* by Paul Westman (Lerner, 1980)

◆ *Space Challenger: The Story of Guion Bluford* by Jim Haskins and Kathleen Benson (Carolrhoda, 1984)

◆ *Twenty Names in Space Exploration* by Brian Williams (Marshall Cavendish, 1990)

◆ *Women in Space* by Carole S. Briggs (Lerner, 1988)

◆ *Women Astronauts Aboard the Shuttle* by Mary Virginia Fox (Simon & Schuster, 1987)

YURI GAGARIN ✷ FIRST PERSON IN SPACE ✷

Yuri Gagarin (1934–1968)

Born: March 9, 1934, in Klushino, Russia
Education: Engineering
Spaceflights: Pilot of *Vostok I* in 1961

AMAZING COSMONAUT INFO:

◆ Fighter pilot in the Soviet Air Force.

◆ Was in the first group of Soviet cosmonauts.

◆ In 1961, flew into space, orbited Earth once. He was the first person in space. and the first in orbit.

◆ Trainer of the women-cosmonaut program.

◆ Died when a jet in which he was training crashed, in 1968.

◆ A Moon crater was named after him.

VALERY POLYAKOV ✷ PERSON SPENDING MOST DAYS IN SPACE ✷

Valery Polyakov (1942–)

Born: April 27, 1942, in Tula, Russia
Education: Medicine
Spaceflights: *Soyuz TM-6/5* to and from space station *Mir* in 1988 and 1994–1995

AMAZING COSMONAUT INFO:

◆ He is a doctor specializing in how the heart and lungs work.

◆ In 1988, flew to space station *Mir* to check on the other cosmonauts.

◆ Studied how the human body deals with weightlessness and the stress of space travel.

◆ Returned to Earth in 1995 after spending a record year and 10 weeks (437 days) in space on *Mir*. No one else has spent such a long time in space.

◆ He said he stayed so long to prove that humans can make it to Mars.

KATHRYN SULLIVAN ✵ FIRST U.S. WOMAN TO WALK IN SPACE ✵

Kathryn Sullivan (1951–)

Born: Oct. 3, 1951, in Paterson, New Jersey
Education: B.S., earth science; Ph.D., geology
Spaceflights: Mission specialist of space shuttles *Challenger* in 1984, *Discovery* in 1990, and *Atlantis* in 1992

AMAZING ASTRONAUT INFO:

◆ She dreamed of being an astronaut after seeing Moon landings as a teenager.

◆ As a scientist, studied the oceans aboard ships—good training for an astronaut.

◆ Speaks six languages.

◆ On October 11, 1984, she and fellow astronaut David Leestma left the shuttle in spacesuits to fix a satellite. She became the first U.S. woman to walk in space.

◆ Left NASA in 1992 to be chief scientist at the National Oceanic and Atmospheric Administration.

JOHN GLENN ✵ FIRST U.S. ASTRONAUT IN ORBIT ✵

John Glenn (1921–)

Born: July 18, 1921, in Cambridge, Ohio
Education: B.S., chemical engineering
Spaceflights: Command pilot of *Mercury–Atlas 6* in 1962

AMAZING ASTRONAUT INFO:

◆ Marine fighter pilot in the Korean War.

◆ Was the first man to fly faster than sound from New York to Los Angeles in 1957. It took five hours.

◆ Was one of the *Mercury 7,* the first group of U.S. astronauts.

◆ Became first American to orbit Earth in 1962.

◆ Elected to U.S. Senate in 1974.

◆ Ran for president in 1984.

VALENTINA TERESHKOVA ✷ FIRST WOMAN IN SPACE ✷

Valentina Tereshkova (1937–)

Born: March 6, 1937, in Maslennikovo, Russia
Education: Engineering
Spaceflights: Pilot of *Vostok 6*

AMAZING COSMONAUT INFO:

◆ Was a parachutist and factory worker.

◆ Wrote the government and asked to be in the space program.

◆ First woman in space. Her trip lasted about 3 days, making 45 orbits around Earth.

◆ Women-cosmonaut program as a separate group ended in 1969.

◆ Worked in the women's movement.

◆ Elected to the Congress of People's Deputies in 1989.

GUION BLUFORD ✷ FIRST U.S. AFRICAN AMERICAN MAN IN SPACE ✷

Guion Bluford (1942–)

Born: November 22, 1942, in Philadelphia, Pennsylvania
Education: B.S., M.S., Ph.D., aerospace engineering; M.B.A.
Spaceflights: Mission specialist on space shuttle *Challenger* in 1983 and 1985, and space shuttle *Discovery* in 1991 and 1992

AMAZING ASTRONAUT INFO:

◆ His high school counselor said he wasn't smart enough for college. But he went anyway and earned many degrees.

◆ Fighter pilot in the U.S. Air Force. Flew 144 combat missions and received 10 medals during Vietnam War.

◆ Chosen with the eighth group of astronauts in 1978. Only 35 people were picked from more than 8,000 applicants.

◆ Has flown on Spacelab, satellite installation, and military space shuttle missions.

SALLY RIDE
✳ FIRST U.S. WOMAN IN SPACE ✳

Sally Ride (1951–)

Born: May 26, 1951, in Los Angeles, California
Education: B.S., M.S., Ph.D., physics; B.A., English
Spaceflights: Mission specialist on space shuttle *Challenger* in 1983 and 1984.

AMAZING ASTRONAUT INFO:

◆ First woman U.S. astronaut.

◆ Was the flight engineer on her first shuttle flight. She made sure everything was working.

◆ Became an astronaut in 1978.

◆ Researched high-energy lasers in college.

◆ Used the shuttle's robotic arm to put satellites into space.

◆ Investigated the *Challenger* accident for President Ronald Reagan

◆ Left NASA to be a full-time scientist.

◆ She could have been a professional tennis player.

NEIL ARMSTRONG ✳ FIRST PERSON TO WALK ON THE MOON ✳

Neil Armstrong (1930–)

Born: August 5, 1930, in Wapakoneta, Ohio
Education: B.S., aeronautical engineering; M.S., aerospace engineering
Spaceflights: Command pilot of *Gemini 8* in 1966 and Commander of *Apollo 11* in 1969

AMAZING ASTRONAUT INFO:

◆ Received his pilot's license on 16th birthday.

◆ Flew combat missions in the Korean War and earned three medals.

◆ As a test pilot he flew X-15 jets at 4,000 mph.

◆ Chosen with the second group of astronauts in 1962.

◆ First civilian astronaut.

◆ Piloted the first docking, or link-up, of two spacecraft in 1966.

◆ First person to walk on the Moon in 1969. "That's one small step for a man, one giant leap for mankind," said Armstrong.

HARRISON SCHMITT ✲ FIRST SCIENTIST ON THE MOON ✲

Harrison Schmitt (1935–)

Born: July 3, 1935, in Santa Rita, New Mexico
Education: B.S., science; Ph.D., geology
Spaceflights: Lunar module pilot of *Apollo 17* in 1972

AMAZING ASTRONAUT INFO:

- Trained astronauts to collect Moon rocks before NASA chose him as an astronaut candidate in 1965.
- In first NASA scientist-astronaut group.
- Ninth person to walk on the Moon. First and only scientist on the Moon.
- Helped collect 243 pounds of Moon rocks and dust during his three-day Moon stay.
- Served one term as U.S. Senator, from 1977 to 1983.

JOHN YOUNG ✲ FIRST SPACE SHUTTLE COMMANDER ✲

John Young (1930–)

Born: Sept. 24, 1930, in San Francisco, California
Education: B.S., aeronautical engineering
Spaceflights: Pilot of *Gemini 3* in 1965, command pilot of *Gemini 10* in 1966, command module pilot of *Apollo 10* in 1969, commander of *Apollo 16* in 1972, commander of space shuttle *Columbia* in 1981 and 1983.

AMAZING ASTRONAUT INFO:

- First person to fly in space six times.
- Was a Navy fighter pilot and test pilot, rank of captain.
- Was on the Moon almost three whole days during *Apollo 16* mission. He collected rocks, drove the Moon rover, and spent 20 hours on Moonwalks.
- Commander of first U.S. space shuttle flight and first shuttle Spacelab mission.
- Grew up near Cape Canaveral in Florida.

★ ★

About an Astronaut

Name _____

Date born _____ Place born _____

What did this astronaut study at school and college? _____

_____

What year did this person become an astronaut? _____

What spacecraft has this astronaut flown in? _____

_____

How many missions has this astronaut flown? _____

What jobs did this astronaut do in space? _____

_____

_____

Interesting information about this astronaut _____

_____

_____

_____

_____

EXTRA: Why do you think she/he wanted to become an astronaut? _____

_____

_____

_____

Neil Armstrong: To the Moon!

by Timothy Nolan

CHARACTERS (in order of appearance)

NARRATOR 1
NARRATOR 2
NASA COMMANDER
NEIL ARMSTRONG, *Apollo 11* astronaut
JANET ARMSTRONG, Neil's wife

EDWIN "BUZZ" ALDRIN, *Apollo 11* astronaut
MICHAEL COLLINS, *Apollo 11* astronaut
TECHNICIAN
VOICE OF MISSION CONTROL

ACT 1   *January 1969. An office at Mission Control. The NASA commander sits at his desk. Neil Armstrong is standing in front of the desk.*

NARRATOR 1: In 1961, President John F. Kennedy told the American people that he wanted the United States to land a man on the Moon by 1970. To accomplish this, the National Aeronautics and Space Administration (NASA) created *Project Mercury,* the first space-flight program. *Project Mercury* put the first Americans in space. It was so successful that NASA started *Project Gemini* to test many of the spaceships and procedures that would be used in a launch to the Moon. One of the astronauts who tested these ships was Neil Armstrong.

NARRATOR 2: On March 16, 1966, he and crewman David Scott successfully docked *Gemini 8* with an orbiting spacecraft. Suddenly, after disconnecting, *Gemini 8* spun out of control! The radio, the astronauts' only connection to Earth, also went dead. Armstrong took the controls and successfully piloted *Gemini 8* back to Earth. He was awarded a medal for his skillful flying.

NARRATOR 1: More challenges lay ahead for Neil Armstrong.

COMMANDER: We've chosen Mike Collins as the pilot for *Apollo 11* and Buzz Aldrin as the specialist, but we still don't have a commander for the crew.

NEIL: Well, sir, I know a lot of good pilots who could do the job.

COMMANDER: I want you to command the flight.

NEIL: Me?!

COMMANDER: We saw how you handled *Gemini 8.* You saved your life and David's. You brought the ship back. Your work has allowed *Project Apollo* to succeed—so far. Now it's time to do what we set out to do—put a man on the Moon. We'd like you to be that man, Neil.

NEIL: Sir, I'm a civilian. I'm not in the military.

COMMANDER: I need the best pilot in the world for this trip. That's you. We need you, Neil. Your country needs you.

NEIL: *(thinks a moment)* I would be honored, sir.

ACT 2 SCENE 1 *July 15, 1969. The astronauts' quarters—Neil and his two Apollo 11 crewmen, Michael Collins and Buzz Aldrin, are inside. Neil is on the phone with his wife, Janet.*

NARRATOR 1: Ten days before the launch of *Apollo 11,* the crew was isolated. They couldn't have any visitors. Food was brought to them by people wearing special suits. Mission briefings were done through glass.

NARRATOR 2: NASA wasn't worried about the crew backing out. They didn't want Armstrong, Collins, and Aldrin going to the Moon with sore throats.

NARRATOR 1: The men's only contact with their families was by telephone.

NEIL: How are the boys?

JANET: They're fine. They miss you, though. I do too.

NEIL: I miss you all too. I wish sometimes they'd picked someone else to command the mission.

JANET: They couldn't. They needed the best pilot. That's you.

NEIL: I don't know about "best."

JANET: I can see the Moon from the living-room window. It's so strange to think that you'll be there soon.

(The NASA commander enters. He is wearing a special protective suit.)

NEIL: The commander just came in, honey. I have to go.

JANET: I'll be looking for you on the Moon. Just make sure you come back home safe and sound.

NEIL: I will. I promise. *(Neil hangs up the phone. He joins the others.)*

COMMANDER: How are you fellows doing?

BUZZ: Great!

MIKE: Terrific!

NEIL: Fine. Ready to fly.

COMMANDER: Good. I just came in to tell you that a landing site on the Moon has been selected. It's a large crater called the Sea of Tranquillity.

BUZZ: Lucky for us there's no water in it!

COMMANDER: It's a huge crater, as wide as a football field and several miles long. It looks smooth enough for a lunar landing. Mike, you'll stay in the command module and orbit the Moon. Neil and Buzz, you'll fly the *Eagle* and land it down in the Sea of Tranquillity. The computer will guide you to the landing point.

NEIL: I thought we were going to fly it down.

COMMANDER: Well, of course, you and Buzz will monitor the computer, but it'll be doing the actual flying. We need you to land at that exact spot. It looks like there aren't any large rocks there.

BUZZ: Rocks are a problem?

COMMANDER: They could break one of the *Eagle's* legs or make the module fall over on its side when you land. Fellows, if something happens to the *Eagle,* there's no way we can rescue you. You know that. You'll be stranded on the Moon forever.

NEIL: Don't worry—we'll find a smooth spot.

COMMANDER: Just trust the computer and you'll be fine. Now get some sleep—you lift off in the morning.

SCENE 2 *July 16, 1969. The launch pad at Cape Kennedy. (Cape Canaveral was named for the late President Kennedy at that time.) Neil, Buzz, and Mike are strapped into the command module* Columbia *by a technician.*

TECHNICIAN: You guys OK?

(The three astronauts give the thumbs-up sign.)

NEIL: Ready to go!

TECHNICIAN: OK, guys. Good luck!

(The technician closes and seals the door. He steps backward through another door and closes it.)

MISSION CONTROL: T minus eight seconds…seven…six…five… four…three…two… one…liftoff!

ACT 3 SCENE 1 *July 20, 1969. Aboard* Apollo 11. *Mike is piloting the command module. Neil and Buzz have moved to the* Eagle, *the lunar module.*

NARRATOR 1: With Mike Collins at the controls of the command module, the *Columbia,* Neil Armstrong and Buzz Aldrin climbed into the *Eagle.* Mike would orbit the Moon while Neil and Buzz were on the Moon. They would then fly the *Eagle* back to the *Columbia* and begin the trip home.

NARRATOR 2: Once the *Eagle* detached from the *Columbia,* the lunar module would be on its own. If something went wrong, Neil and Buzz would be lost in space.

NEIL: *Eagle* to *Columbia.* We're on our way.

MIKE: See you both in a couple of days. Have fun on the Moon. Bring me back some green cheese.

BUZZ: Don't go anywhere without us.

NEIL: *Apollo 11* to Mission Control.

MISSION CONTROL: Go ahead, *Apollo 11.*

NEIL: Mission Control, the *Eagle* has wings. We are en route to the Moon.

MISSION CONTROL: Roger, *Eagle.* We are engaging the on-board computer.

NEIL: Roger, Mission Control.

BUZZ: Looks like we get to sit back and enjoy the ride.

NEIL: Let's hope so.

NARRATOR 1: Neil and Buzz monitored their instruments and looked out the window of the *Eagle.* From a distance, the Sea of Tranquillity looked like a large open patch on the lunar landscape. But as the crater got closer, the astronauts saw one large rock. Then another. And another.

BUZZ: Uh-oh. Neil, take a look at this.

NEIL: What is it?

BUZZ: The Sea of Tranquillity—it's full of rocks!

NEIL: Look for a smooth place.

BUZZ: *(looks out the window)* I don't see one, Neil.

NEIL: *Eagle* to Mission Control. Come in, Mission Control.

MISSION CONTROL: Mission Control here.

NEIL: The Sea of Tranquillity is covered with rocks. We cannot land there. Repeat, we cannot land there.

MISSION CONTROL: Continue to monitor the computer, *Eagle.*

NEIL: The computer's leading us into the rocks, Mission Control. Request permission to override and switch to manual control.

MISSION CONTROL: Stand by, *Eagle.* Continue to monitor computer.

BUZZ: We can't do that. Those rocks are getting too close.

NEIL: Cannot do that, Mission Control.

MISSION CONTROL: You do not have enough fuel for manual control, *Eagle.*

BUZZ: Neil, we're getting close. We don't have much time.

NEIL: *Eagle* is switching to manual control, Mission Control.

NARRATOR 2: Neil turned off the computer and took the controls. An alarm immediately went off.

BUZZ: Uh-oh, low fuel alert.

NEIL: How much do we have left?

BUZZ: About two minutes' worth.

NEIL: Mission Control, *Eagle* is now searching for a landing site.

MISSION CONTROL: Fuel is low, *Eagle.*

NEIL: We're aware of that, Mission Control. *(He looks out of the window.)* I think I see a clear spot.

MISSION CONTROL: One minute of fuel left, *Eagle.*

NEIL: Almost there…

MISSION CONTROL: Forty-five seconds…

NEIL: We're over the spot. Fire the retro rockets.

BUZZ: Roger.

MISSION CONTROL: Forty seconds…

NEIL: We're going down.

MISSION CONTROL: *Eagle,* your landing spot may not be firm enough to hold the craft.

NEIL: We have no choice, Mission Control. We're going down.

BUZZ: Almost there, Neil.

MISSION CONTROL: Thirty seconds of fuel left...

NEIL: We're about to touch down.

NARRATOR 1: The *Eagle* landed with a small bump. There is no more movement.

MISSION CONTROL: *Eagle*—are you there?

NEIL: Tranquillity Base here. The *Eagle* has landed.

MISSION CONTROL: Roger, *Eagle.* Nice job. You are now cleared to take a nap for the next four hours—

NEIL AND BUZZ: A nap?

BUZZ: No way! We want to get out there!

NEIL: Mission Control, request permission to explore the surface of the Moon.

MISSION CONTROL: You two should rest—

NEIL: We didn't fly to the Moon to take a nap.

MISSION CONTROL: Permission granted, *Eagle.*

SCENE 2 *Surface of the Moon. Neil, now in his full space suit, steps down the ladder on the side of the* Eagle.

NEIL: I've reached the bottom of the ladder...I'm standing on the pad... I'm now stepping off the pad...*(He steps on the surface of the Moon.)* That's one small step for a man, one giant leap for mankind.

MISSION CONTROL: How does it look, Commander?

NEIL: Dark...there are some rocks...lots of desolation.

MISSION CONTROL: Not much out there, huh, Commander?

NEIL: No, but it's beautiful.

NARRATOR 2: After a few minutes, Buzz joined Neil on the Moon's surface. They took soil samples, performed scientific experiments, and planted an American flag. After about two and a half hours, the two men went back into the *Eagle* and successfully flew back to the *Columbia.* All three astronauts returned safely to Earth on July 24, 1969. President Richard Nixon flew halfway around the world to greet them. A huge ticker-tape parade was held in their honor in New York City. The astronauts' next trips were tamer: they visited a total of 22 countries and were greeted by thousands of people. The next year, Neil Armstrong retired from NASA. His footprints are still visible on the surface of the Moon.

My Training Program

Astronauts train tough to make it into space. But they don't have to be superstrong, just in shape. A physically fit body better withstands the stress of space travel. See how much training can help you improve your own personal fitness.

1 Pick an exercise. Here are some examples: sit-ups, push-ups, walking up and down stairs, chair stepping. It has to be something you can count. Write the exercise on the chart.

2 Time how many you can do in five minutes. Set a timer, or have a parent or friend time you. Write the number on the chart.

3 Practice! For the next week practice your exercise every day.

4 When a week has passed, repeat step 2.

5 Repeat step 2 again after a second, third, and fourth week. Did you improve?

My exercise is	Date	Number of exercises I did...
today		
after 1 week		
after 2 weeks		
after 3 weeks		
after 4 weeks		

EXTRA: Now that you know how much you can improve, set a goal for a month from now and repeat.

CHAPTER 5

FUTURE JOURNEYS

The Next Steps

What will be the next great achievements in space science, and where will they take us? The U.S., Germany, and other countries are trying to improve on the space shuttle design with an *aerospace plane*. It wouldn't need to blast off like a rocket and lose boosters as it climbed. Space probes will also continue to do the far-flung exploring for now. We still have much to learn not only about building a craft to take humans far beyond our moon but also how to survive en route and once we arrive. In 1989, President George Bush set the goals in this order: first, building a space station; second, building a Moon outpost; and third, sending an astronaut mission to Mars. Whether it is NASA, private American industries, foreign governments, or international corporations that accomplish these goals is yet to be determined. But with the Cold War over, global technological advances, and fewer government blank checks for space projects, it seems likely that international cooperation will be a feature of most future space journeys.

A case in point is the current international effort to build an orbiting space station. Led by the United States, the construction of the International Space Station is tentatively slated to begin in late 1997. Russia is responsible for the first step. It will send up a spacecraft that will provide propulsion, docking equipment, and fuel storage in

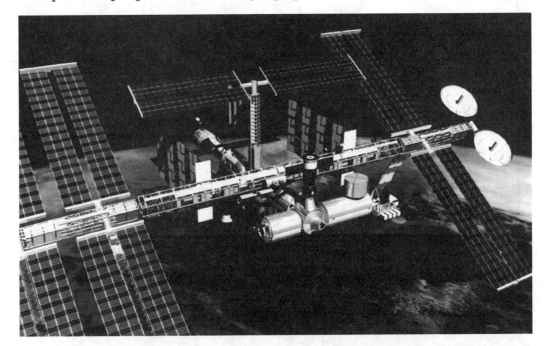

International Space Station, phase III

November of 1997. A U.S. space shuttle will carry up the U.S. laboratory module and other lab equipment in the first half of 1998. (U.S. lab and living quarters modules are each 14.5 feet in diameter and 27 feet long.) The space station will then be ready to start microgravity experiments. However, whoever runs or maintains these experiments will have to stay on a docked spacecraft. Starting in late 1998, a crew will be able to work on the station independent of another craft. Supplies and crews will be shuttled up and back. Japan steps in during the year 2000 with a robotic arm it's developing and its own module for attachment. The European Space Agency plans to deliver its lab module in 2001. Expanded crew living quarters are on the delivery timetable for 2002, when the station will be able to permanently house six people. Two Russian rescue vehicles will stay at the station and the U.S. space shuttles will ferry crews and supplies.

Artist's representation of a Moon outpost

No one has been on the Moon since 1972. But an outpost on the Moon seems inevitable to many space scientists. They see the Moon as the perfect place to practice and develop technologies for surviving on another world. A colony can be shuttled up little by little over a number of years. Colonists might live in sealed modules or domes, extract oxygen from the soil for air and rocket fuel, eat plants grown in greenhouses, and mine the Moon's minerals. It's only a few days' travel to the space station or Earth, if problems occur. The Moon is also closer to another destination, Mars.

> ### FAST FACT
> Some scientists believe that one day humans may have the technology to change the climate, or *terraform*, of Mars to suit human needs.

Mars is our most similar neighbor—add more air, increase the temperature, and it'd be much like Earth. It has ice caps, canyons, and channels that may once have been riverbeds. Was there once life on Mars? Did it once have a more Earth-like climate? These Martian mysteries and others are reasons people want to send a crewed mission to explore the red planet. At current space-traveling speeds, it's a two-year round-trip to Mars. A spaceship to Mars would probably orbit the planet once it arrived, sending landing modules to the surface, much as the *Apollo* missions did with the Moon. Outposts on the two Martian moons are also possible. These moons, Phobos and Deimos, are probably captured asteroids and may have minerals and ice that could be made into water, air, and rocket fuel. It seems that what little we have learned about Mars has only fueled a desire by Earth's inhabitants to arrange a visit.

ACTIVITIES

Design a Space Station
(Science and Society)

The International Space Station has undergone many design changes since its original inception and its stint as space station *Freedom*. Chances are this station won't be alone for long. There will probably be more space stations built in the future, especially as demand grows for materials and equipment that are developed, manufactured, and tested in space. Help students think of possibilities for future space stations by having them design their own stations.

Start a class discussion about how a space station might be used someday. Mention experimenting with ways to grow food in space, how the body reacts to space, how machinery works in space, etc. Also discuss that it might be used as a way station to points beyond as a giant solar collector to produce energy for the station and/or Earth, or as a defense system against rogue asteroids and comets. How would it be built? From material shuttled from Earth or the Moon colony? Would spacewalkers do the construction or robots? Let students brainstorm. Pictures of possible designs from the library or books will help. Next, distribute a copy of page 77 to student pairs or small groups. First they need to decide on a station name and what its purpose would be and fill out the form. (Construction date is far in the future!) Then they need to draw and label a "blueprint" of their station.

EXTENSION ACTIVITY Instead of drawing their stations, challenge students to make three-dimensional models out of clay, cardboard, paper-towel tubes, plastic soft-drink bottles, and other materials. Have each student group explain their designs to the class and field questions about what their station can and can't do.

To Go or Not to Go? (Language Arts)

A Moon outpost or colony seems inevitable. What would life be like on the Moon? Would students want to live there? Start a class discussion about how they think people would live—in sealed domes, eating food from greenhouses, with less gravity, and working in mines. Let students debate why they would like to live on the Moon and why they wouldn't.

EXTENSION ACTIVITY Students' views on going to the Moon or not make good subjects for persuasive written essays.

Application for Space Corps
(Science, Language Arts)

Maybe young people in the future will join a space corps instead of the military or Peace Corps. Now that they know something about what life might be like on the Moon, Mars, and space stations in the not-too-distant future, let students sign up to go! Distribute a copy of page 78 to each student. Then let them all fill out their application.

EXTENSION ACTIVITY Assign a selection committee to choose volunteers for service for each space destination.

SCIENCE TO GO ➠ Space Survey
(Science and Society)

Space can be controversial. Many people were against the goal of landing on the Moon in the 1960s. They argued that the tens of billions of tax dollars could be better spent on education, infrastructure, or the poor. And the debate continues. In the 1990s, Congress has repeatedly cut funding for NASA in general and the space station in particular. What do students, their families, and friends think about the space program and its goals? Distribute a copy of page 79 to students to take home and do their own Space Survey.

CULMINATING ACTIVITIES (Cross-Curricular)

Help students synthesize all they've learned during their space unit with a few of the following activities.

◆ **Space Debates** Students can research and present their views on hot space topics like: Should we build a Moon base? Will people live on Mars? The survey questions on page 79 all make good debate topics.

◆ **Space Comic Books** Challenge students to make a comic book about a great event in space history like the Moon landing (see the play on pages 66–70), the first human in orbit, or the first shuttle launch. Space Milestones on pages 32–33 is a great place to start when looking for space events.

◆ **Space Current Events** Start a class bulletin board for Space in the News. Invite students to bring in newspaper and magazine clippings about space topics—from the latest shuttle missions and newest photos from the Hubble Space Telescope to which planets are easily seen this week (often in the weather section of daily newspapers).

◆ **Class Trip!** Arrange a class trip to a local planetarium, space center, cosmosphere, or aviation or science museum.

◆ **Design Space Equipment** Challenge students to design a piece of needed space equipment—anything from a better grabbing spoon to a Mars rover.

◆ **Life-size Spaceship** Students can build a life-size replica of an early *Mercury, Gemini,* or *Apollo* capsule using cardboard boxes and papier-mâché.

◆ **Rocket History Time Line** Trace the growing size of rockets over time by having students make to-scale drawings of different rockets and arranging them along a wall as a time line.

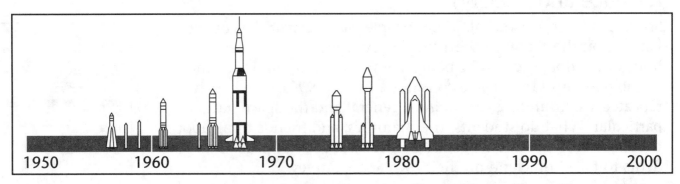

| 1950 | 1960 | 1970 | 1980 | 1990 | 2000 |

◆ **Space Newsletter** Have the class publish a *Space Times* newsletter complete with space stories, a space crossword puzzle, and an editorial section.

◆ **Astronomer Biographies** Astronauts aren't the only heroes in the history of space. Astronomers are scientists who help us view and explore the farthest reaches of our universe. Invite students to research and report on a particular astronomer.

BOOK LINKS

Classroom/Teacher Reference Books

◆ *Cambridge Encyclopedia of Space* edited by Michael Rycroft (University of Cambridge Press, 1990)

Books for Independent Reading

◆ *Living in Space* by Larry Kettelkamp (Morrow Junior Books, 1993)

◆ *The Day We Walked on the Moon* by George Sullivan (Scholastic, 1990)

Names _____

★ ★

Design a Space Station

NAME _____

OUR COMPANY/GOVERNMENT NAME _____

STATION CONSTRUCTION DATES _____

How many people will live there _____

What our station will do _____

_____

_____

_____

Application for Space Corps

SUMMER OF 2025

Your name _____

Earth country _____

Where do you want to go?
Please make a first [1] and second [2] choice.

☐ Moon colony   ☐ Space station

☐ Martian moon colony   ☐ Mars planet colony

Why do you want to go to your *first* choice? _____

_____

_____

_____

_____

Why do you want to go to your *second* choice? _____

_____

_____

_____

_____

Why are you a good Space Corps candidate? _____

_____

_____

_____

_____

Name _____

★ ★

SCIENCE TO GO⟶

Space Survey

What do you, your family, friends, and neighbors think about space? Should we spend a lot of money and get to Mars as quickly as we can? Or are there more important things to spend money on these days? Find out by taking a survey.

First find someone to survey. Then ask the person each question below (write in two more questions of your own) and put a tally mark under Yes or No. The next person's answers go in the same places. When you're finished, add up the tallies to get the results.

QUESTIONS	YES	NO
1 Was sending a human to the Moon a good thing?		
2 Should NASA build a space station as part of an international project with other countries?		
3 Do you think NASA should send astronauts to Mars?		
4		
5		

EXTRA: Draw a graph or pie chart of your survey results.

BIBLIOGRAPHY

Astronaut Training by Ann Armbruster and Elizabeth A. Taylor (Franklin Watts, 1990)

Astronomy by Roy A. Gallant (Macmillian, 1986)

Atlas of Stars and Planets by Ian Ridpath (Facts on File, 1993)

Cambridge Encyclopedia of Space edited by Michael Rycroft (University of Cambridge Press, 1990)

The Day We Walked on the Moon by George Sullivan (Scholastic, 1990)

The Dream Is Alive by Barbara Embury (HarperCollins, 1990)

Eclipse by Franklyn M. Branley (HarperCollins, 1988)

Exploring the Night Sky by Terrance Dickinson (Camden House, 1987)

Exploring the Sky: 100 Projects for Beginning Astronomers by Richard Moeschl (Chicago Review, 1989)

Flying the Space-shuttles by Don Dwiggins (Dodd, Mead, & Co., 1985)

Galaxies and Quasars by Heather Couper (Franklin Watts, 1986)

John Glenn: Astronaut and Senator by Michael D. Cole (Enslow, 1993)

John Young: Space-shuttle Commander by Paul Westman (Dillion Press, 1981)

Living in Space by Don Berliner (Lerner, 1993)

Living in Space by Larry Kettelkamp (Morrow Junior Books, 1993)

The Magic School Bus Lost in the Solar System by Joanna Cole (Scholastic, 1990)

The Moon Seems to Change by Franklyn M. Branley (HarperCollins, 1987)

My Place in Space by Robin and Sally Hirst (Orchard Books, 1990)

The Moon by Seymour Simon (MacMillian, 1984)

Neil Armstrong by Paul Westman (1980, Lerner)

The Nova Space Explorer's Guide: Where to Go and What to See by Richard Maurer (Clarkson Potter, 1985)

One Giant Leap by Mary Ann Fraser (Henry Holt, 1993)

The Planets in Our Solar System by Franklyn M. Branley (HarperCollins, 1981)

Planets, Moons and Meteors by John R. Gustafson (RGA, 1992)

Rockets: Physical Science Teacher's Guide with Activities by NASA Education Division (NASA, 1993)

Space Almanac edited by Anthony R. Curtis (Gulf, 1992)

Space Challenger: The Story of Guion Bluford by Jim Haskins and Kathleen Benson (Carolrhoda, 1984)

Space Probes to the Planets by Fay Robinson (Albert Whitman, 1993)

The Space-shuttle by George S. Fichter (Franklin Watts, 1990)

Spacecraft by N. S. Barrett (Franklin Watts, 1985)

Stargazers by Gail Gibbons (Holiday House, 1992)

Twenty Names in Space Exploration by Brian Williams (Marshall Cavendish, 1990)

U.S. Space Gear: Outfitting the Astronaut by Lilian D. Kozloski (Smithsonian Institution Press, 1994)

What the Moon Is Like by Franklyn M. Branley (HarperCollins, 1986)

Women Astronauts Aboard the Shuttle by Mary Virginia Fox (Simon & Schuster, 1987)

Women in Space by Carole S. Briggs (Lerner, 1988)

Zero Gravity by Gloria Skurzynski (Bradbury, 1994)